The fact that men need friendships is not an accident. God made us that way. A man without real friends is a man vulnerable, discouraged, and spiritually unhappy. In this book, you will learn about the friendships a man needs—and why this matters so much to Christians.

Dr. R. Albert Mohler, Jr.
President, The Southern Baptist Theological Seminary, Louisville, KY

I love Justin's word picture of the kid who climbs up the playground slide to come down rather than using the steps. I see so much of this in the world of sports that I'm involved in—the pursuit of the quick fix, the instant results. But as a disciple of Christ, there are vital steps of patience that must be taken in maturing faith. I love this Gospel-centric reminder of the need for us to take the steps of patience in being discipled by mentors and discipling others for King Jesus.

Ron Brown
Director of Player Development,
University of Nebraska Football
Cofounder and codirector of Kingdom Sports

Following Jesus and serving my family are my first two passions in life. Racing and race cars are third. My uncle was a racer, so this passion developed while growing near our local dirt track. Justin's book had me hooked from the first page. Using the elements of racing—from the crew chief and every person on the pit crew and even the spectators—to illustrate what a man needs in his life was spot on! This book, while written for men, can definitely apply to women as well. After all, lots of women love Jesus and sports!

Janet Hunt
Wife of Dr. Johnny Hunt,
former senior pastor of First Baptist Church Woodstock, Georgia

Having a front-row seat to history and serving one of the greatest leaders of our era, President Ronald Reagan, I saw the value of being surrounded by people who support, encourage, and challenge you. Many of Reagan's achievements wouldn't have been possible without friends and advisers who helped him be strong and successful while still maintaining his faith, his marriage to Nancy, and his visionary patriotism and optimism. *Seven Friendships Every Man Needs* provides you with a road map for staying on the path toward a successful life, meaningful friendships, and godly excellence.

Peggy Grande
Executive Assistant to President Ronald Reagan, 1989–1999

Someone has said that a friend is someone who walks in when everyone else walks out. Justin articulates well what that kind of friend looks like in *Seven Friendships Every Man Needs*. There are friends who stick closer than a brother. Find a friend, and be a friend.

Ken Whitten
Pastor, Idlewild Baptist Church
Tampa Bay, Florida

7 FRIENDSHIPS EVERY MAN NEEDS

JUSTIN ERICKSON

HARVEST HOUSE PUBLISHERS
EUGENE, OREGON

Cover by Kyler Dougherty

Cover photos © Patthana Nirangkul, Sawadast, southtownboy / Getty

Seven Friendships Every Man Needs
Copyright © 2019 Justin Erickson
Published by Harvest House Publishers
Eugene, Oregon 97408
www.harvesthousepublishers.com

ISBN 978-0-7369-7514-8 (pbk.)
ISBN 978-0-7369-7515-5 (eBook)

Library of Congress Cataloging-in-Publication Data

Names: Erickson, Justin, 1974- author.
Title: Seven friendships every man needs / Justin Erickson.
Description: Eugene, Oregon : Harvest House Publishers, [2018]
Identifiers: LCCN 2018023300 (print) | LCCN 2018041878 (ebook) | ISBN 9780736975155 (ebook) | ISBN 9780736975148 (pbk.)
Subjects: LCSH: Christian men--Conduct of life. | Male friendship--Religious aspects--Christianity.
Classification: LCC BV4528.2 (ebook) | LCC BV4528.2 .E75 2018 (print) | DDC 241/.67620811--dc23
LC record available at https://lccn.loc.gov/2018023300

Printed in the United States of America

19 20 21 22 23 24 25 26 27 / VP-GL / 10 9 8 7 6 5 4 3 2 1

To James Keasling,
a man of character who has shaped me by imparting
the courageous conviction of Daniel,
the practical wisdom of Solomon,
and the tender affection of the father I never had.

Acknowledgments

Who knew that writing a book would be this fun? Who imagined that writing a book would be this much work? I certainly did not. I graduated high school without having ever read a single book, the single chapter in any book, and to the best of my knowledge, I never even finished one newspaper article. This book then is a testament to the shaping influence of others, who I would be remiss if I failed to acknowledge.

First, special thanks to Bob Hawkins of Harvest House Publishers, who extended the invitation for me to write this book several years ago and has waited patiently for its completion. His team has made this process enjoyable and smooth.

To Russell Taylor, my first mentor, who started discipling me when I was two months old in the Lord—his influence permeates every page of this volume. He set the standard for all the mentors I have ever let into my life since.

To my wife, Jana, who has not only supported me feverishly in this project, but who herself embodies all the qualities of the friendships described herein.

To my children, Emma, Ashlyn, Ty, Janie, and Allie, who intuitively knew when to give me time and space to write, and when it was time to interrupt and rescue me.

Finally, I owe an immeasurable debt of gratitude to Steve Miller, whose expert instruction, relentless encouragement, and tireless commitment to me and this book has been like a Masterclass. Every author needs a Steve. Words fall short.

Contents

What It Takes to Thrive as a Man

This book is about guys and how we do friendships. Honestly, I'm not sure we're great at it. We do have friends, even good ones, but guys get a bum rap when it comes to our relationships with other men. Our friendships have a stigma. We get critiqued because our conversations almost always tend toward work, sports, weekend hobbies, and mango-habanero buffalo wings long before we delve into something spiritual and eternal.

I joke with my wife because often in ministry contexts, I will be walking past her and overhear a woman approaching her and saying, "Hi! My name is Jana—good to meet you…" Then I'll walk by again ten minutes later and see that same woman crying and disclosing the darkest secrets hidden in the caverns of her soul. I stand there amazed and just shake my head. All I had achieved in those ten minutes amounted to a half-pint of guacamole, a mound of chips, and a couple YouTube videos about flyboarding (which is awesome, by the way).

Now, while I would be the first to admit that I have contributed to our collective reputation as men, I used to think that we are just lame and need to do friendships like women do friendships. I don't think that anymore. Nor should you.

Here's a different angle: We are not women; we are men. Profound, I know.

But as men, we relate to each other differently than women relate to women. That, I believe, is by *design*. When Paul told the believers in Corinth to "act like men" (1 Corinthians 16:13), he also provided descriptions of that manhood: A man is watchful, stands firm in the truth, is strong, and does everything in love. We were created to be out in front, so that we might use our strength to protect, guide, and nurture those who look to us. In a sense, we were created to be independent. That's not to say that we don't need helpers. I'm pretty sure that's why Genesis 2 is in the Bible. God made us to need our wives, but a wife serves a different role in our lives than the other men around us. It is other men who can help us be the man God made us to be.

Notice I didn't say that we are self-sufficient. Independence and self-sufficiency aren't the same thing. Self-sufficient men are arrogant, self-willed, unteachable, and manipulative. By contrast, independent men may start out alone, but they know how to bring other men into their lives who can help them. They are intentional about friendships and know how to use them for good.

Women look to men for security, vision, direction, protection, and provision. We don't look to each other for that. *We help each other be that for those who look to us.*

King David affirmed this truth on the day he took office, when he said in Psalm 101:6, "My eyes shall be upon the faithful of the land, that they may dwell with me; he who walks in a blameless way is the one who will minister to me." He knew that vital to his integrity was the encouragement, accountability, and strength of strong guy friends. This was at least one of the reasons that he was a man after God's own heart. Men get men, and this book is written to show you how to find and leverage those relationships for what's most important.

Specifically, I believe that within the course of your life, there are a small handful of friendships you need. Seven, to be exact. That's all—just seven. You can have more. In fact, you can have as many as you want. But you need at least these seven guys in your life. They are illustrated by the friendships modeled for us in the Bible.

I believe every man needs a Paul, a mentor who can disciple you like he did Timothy. If that's true, every man needs a Timothy, a disciple who will follow your life and doctrine. Yet no man can be without a Barnabas, a peer to come alongside and encourage you in the midst of your highs and lows. At times, you need a Nathan, like King David had—a brave spiritual brother who can challenge and rebuke you when you get out of line. Most men long for—but few have—a Jonathan. Like David's best friend, you can have a loyal kindred to strengthen you when your world is closing in. Of course you can never overlook your need for a Zacchaeus, a lost sinner who needs to hear the gospel as well as see what God has done in you— you're coming to his house today. These relationships are critical because they ultimately help you in the relationship that matters most: the One who personified manhood perfectly—Jesus Christ.

Simply put, you need guy friends. God made us to be relational. He is relational. The Bible is clear that we grow in relationship with others. Rarely will you find, in God's Word, an example of someone flourishing on his own. And while our relationships aren't perfect, if you have these seven in your life, you will thrive as a man.

You are like a high-performance race car, and your guy friends are like your pit crew. You are a leader, which means you are high-octane.

You need guy friends.
God made us to be relational.
He is relational. The Bible is
clear that we grow in
relationship with others.
Rarely will you find, in
God's Word, an example
of someone flourishing
on his own.

You go fast and are a peak performer who wants to win. The men described for you in this book are the team that comes over the wall, each man with his own special role in your life. They are there to get you back on track and across the finish line. Your crew chief steers you around obstacles. Your jack-man jacks up the vehicle so you can get new tires. Your tire-changer gives you new tires so you don't have a blowout. The fuel man is always ready with the gas pump to ensure your tank is full. Your fire extinguisher keeps you from getting burned to a crisp. The crowd in the stands is watching every turn you make, and the trophy is waiting for you just past the checkered flag. You have to get across that line. You need a pit crew. As you turn the next page, you're coming off the track for your first pit stop.

CHAPTER 1

You Need a Godly Mentor to Disciple You

This book is about having a select group of men in your life who are committed to your personal spiritual victory. I've invited you to think of yourself as a high-performance race car and your life as a track. Like NASCAR drivers, men are generally intense, go hard, and are high-octane. We love a challenge and crave a victory.

If you've ever been to an auto race, you know the smell of exhaust and burnt rubber. It's probably toxic, but exhilarating. It's electrifying to watch the cars warm up and the drivers do their final checks. Everyone's adrenaline surges when the cars line up at the start with motors revving. Every driver who waits for the green light has a mental picture of himself crossing the finish line first. He thinks about it every day. He is also aware that it takes almost nothing to spin out—and that doing so could cost him the race, his career, or even his life. If he gets too close to another car or doesn't hold the proper tension on the wheel, it could be over before he realizes it.

I want you to finish well, spiritually speaking. Many guys do finish well, but more guys don't. I've seen men spin out, blow out, and flame out. For guys, the most common cause for elimination comes from one of three things: gold, glory, or girls. Gold, the love of money and what it buys. Glory, when pride and ego get in the way. Girls caused the strongest, wisest, and godliest men of the Old Testament to crash and burn (Samson, Solomon, and David respectively).

If you're going to win, you must see that your success on the track of life is not so much a matter of your ability to handle yourself. Every driver whose car has crossed first under the checkered flag knows he didn't win on his own. It wasn't his performance on the track that gave him the victory. It was the men in his pit crew that kept him on the track. They are as much responsible for the win, and maybe even more. There is no victory without them.

In this chapter, I want to speak to you about your crew chief. He's that experienced voice of wisdom in your ear, guiding you throughout the race. He knows the track because he's been on it before and won. He also knows you, your temperaments and impulses as a driver. Because he was once in your seat, he's an expert at when to brake and when to hit the gas. He's also aware of what a race car can and cannot do under intense pressure. He anticipates other drivers' next steps and knows how to navigate you through the harrowing maze of speeding cars all around you.

A crew chief is unlike any other member on the pit team. Everyone has a part and must be fully engaged to ensure a victory, but the crew chief is the most strategic. In racing, he doesn't do everything, but he's instrumental in everything. He oversees the building of the car's body, how the springs and shocks are adjusted, the level of air pressure in the tires—everything. He lives to see you succeed. He lends his knowledge and ability to communicate critical decisions in a split second. His nerves of steel allow him to rise above the pressure and think clearly so you can win. The same is true in the spiritual realm. Your crew chief functions like a coach and manager. He's not the owner. That's Jesus. But Jesus brings him alongside you to help you make some critical decisions in your life. In short, you need a mentor.

The Vital Role of a Mentor

All mentoring relationships are different. There's no "one size fits all." Some relationships are formal, while others are informal. The duration can be short-term or lifelong. Some will be intensely focused on vital issues like conflict, finances, parenting, and ministry. But most are "life-on-life" role models. All of them can say, "Be imitators of me, as I am of Christ" (1 Corinthians 11:1).

You see that variety reflected in the biblical examples of discipleship. Consider Jethro and Moses, Moses and Joshua, or Jesus and the apostles. These examples show that you don't have to limit yourself to one mentoring style or one person. In fact, you shouldn't. No one person perfectly models all the qualities of Christlikeness. Different men have different strengths. At this point in my spiritual journey, I've had the privilege of being mentored by nine different men. Each of them have had a different influence in my life. I saw something of Christ in them that I didn't see in me, and I am more like Jesus because of them.

The best example for our purposes is the one-on-one discipling relationship between Paul and Timothy, which began in Acts 16:

> Paul came also to Derbe and to Lystra. A disciple was there, named Timothy, the son of a Jewish woman who was a believer, but his father was a Greek. He was well spoken of

by the brothers at Lystra and Iconium. Paul wanted Timothy to accompany him, and he took him and circumcised
him because of the Jews who were in those places, for they
all knew that his father was a Greek. As they went on their
way through the cities, they delivered to them for obser-
vance the decisions that had been reached by the apostles
and elders who were in Jerusalem. So the churches were
strengthened in the faith, and they increased in numbers
daily (verses 1-5).

As the story goes, Paul had been looking for a replacement for
John Mark, who at the time turned out to be a colossal failure.
Returning to the region where he had been beaten and stoned,
Paul discovered a young man who had God's hand on him. Timothy possessed certain qualities that Paul sought, and Timothy
was willing and available. It was that simple of a start. Neither
man would ever be the same again. The legacy of Christianity would pass from one generation to the next because of this
connection.

Timothy filled a crucial gap for Paul, and Paul did the same in
return. We learn in the text that Timothy's mom "was a believer,
but his father was a Greek." The contrast is there to help us understand that Timothy did not have a spiritual father. His biological
father was not saved. His mother and grandmother were Jews who
had embraced Jesus as their Messiah (2 Timothy 1:5), but his father
had not. Dad was in the picture, but he was not a Christian.

We don't know much of the backstory, except that the issue
of how to raise Timothy would have caused a conflict. From the
text, we know that Timothy's dad wouldn't let his wife get Timothy circumcised, which was a big deal in Jewish culture. Circumcision was the first display of hope that believing Jewish

parents had for their boys. It identified them with the covenant of Abraham. It came with the prayer that one day their sons would believe in the same God and follow Him. Dad said no, but his mother's prayers were still answered. Timothy eventually became a Christian.

I feel a lot like Timothy in the sense that I never had a dad. My biological dad left when I was born. He didn't want a son. My second dad was enslaved to alcohol. He wasn't a believer and often trashed our house in fits of rage. Tragically, he ended his own life just before he turned 50. I'd give the world to have him back.

But when God saved me, He showed me that He was my true Father. He had allowed me to experience that vacuum so that when I saw my need for God, I would ask Him to fill the gap left by my earthly fathers. Then the Lord saw fit to put other strong men into my life who would mentor me in the areas where I was misshaped as a child. That's what Paul gave to Timothy. He stepped in as a spiritual father and considered Timothy his son in the faith:

> That is why I sent you Timothy, my beloved and faithful child in the Lord, to remind you of my ways in Christ, as I teach them everywhere in every church (1 Corinthians 4:17).

> You know Timothy's proven worth, how as a son with a father he has served with me in the gospel (Philippians 2:22).

That's what you're looking for and need—an older, godlier man with whom you can live out your faith in a real way. But you have to allow him into your life. For you to grow, you will have to let him come at you from four different directions.

Four Key Ways a Mentor Can Help You

Direction #1: Let Him Impart Truth to You

In the New Testament, the word *disciple* means "learner." It means to place yourself under someone else's influence to help you become a better follower of God. A disciple learns truth, but this involves more than just Bible knowledge. You don't know it until you do it. The truth has to own you, and you have own it.

As it relates to your spiritual development, your mentor imparts wisdom and strengthens your convictions. A conviction is a governing principle for life. It centers on divine truth and describes those things that you are deeply persuaded are true. They are realities you would live to proclaim and die to defend. No mentoring is biblical discipleship without the Word of God.

The person you're looking for can teach you sound doctrine and train you to be a student of Scripture. He should know how to handle God's Word and teach you how to understand it for yourself. Your conversations should be able to trace back to "chapter and verse." It doesn't have to be formal, like a sermon, but there should be lots of interaction with the biblical text.

My first mentor, Russell Taylor, did this for me. I grew up in an atheist home and came to Christ with no clue about anything spiritually. All I knew was that Christ had changed my life, but not much else. I didn't know what I didn't know. I was susceptible to any form of false teaching. For the next two years, we spent a lot of time together. We talked about God's Word and I peppered him with questions. His default was, "Well, the Bible says…," and then he would take out his Bible and show me. As he modeled how to interpret the Bible, he then used that to help me interpret the world around me. The more time we spent together, the easier it became for me to figure things out on my own. Simple, but life-changing.

That's what a spiritual mentor offers: exposure to the truth of Scripture, rightly interpreted. You're looking for a Paul, not a penguin. Penguins feed their young in a most interesting way. First they catch the fish and digest them inside their own stomachs for several hours. Then they regurgitate the slimy chunks and deposit them into their chick's beak. Discipleship might be a little bit like that at first, but the goal is to get you to learn how to feed yourself. You want someone to teach you the truth and how to discover it on your own.

Paul did this with Timothy. He labored to instill some spiritual nonnegotiables into his disciple—truths that would hold him long after Paul was gone. You can read many of them in 1 and 2 Timothy, but consider some of Paul's final words to his disciple in 2 Timothy 3:14-17:

> You, however, continue in the things you have learned and become convinced of, knowing from whom you have learned them, and that from childhood you have known the sacred writings which are able to give you the wisdom that leads to salvation through faith which is in Christ Jesus. All Scripture is inspired by God and profitable for teaching, for reproof, for correction, for training in righteousness; so that the man of God may be adequate, equipped for every good work (NASB).

You may already be familiar with verses 16-17, which affirm the importance of God's Word. According to Paul, the Bible does four things for us. First, it teaches us God's standards. Next, it reveals where we fall short of those standards. Third, Scripture puts us back into alignment with His will. And finally, it instills new patterns of righteousness in us. When God's Word has its way with us, we become "adequate, equipped for every good work." The Bible can make each of us "the man of God" He wants us to be.

Notice the context in which that promise was given. It follows a command. Paul told Timothy to "continue in the things you have learned and become convinced of." He was to keep going in the truth, to persevere in godliness. He could do this not only because he had learned "the sacred writings"—lots of people know the Bible. Rather, Timothy could persevere because he had become "convinced of" it. Somewhere along the way, the information he had learned "from childhood" became the beliefs that made him who he was. He knew it, then he owned it. And in 2 Timothy 3:14-17, Paul called upon Timothy to "continue in" the truth.

Now, when Timothy rolled back the rest of Paul's scroll, he learned that Paul was at the end of his life. He was about to die, martyred at the hands of Nero. Soon he would be in heaven. Timothy might never see his mentor again, but the convictions Paul had deposited into Timothy would remain long after Paul was gone. That is, if Timothy could grasp one simple fact: The key to maintaining your convictions is remembering those who imparted them to you.

Paul explained how this happens: "Continue in the things you have learned and become convinced of, knowing from whom you have learned them." See it? Biblical content translates into biblical convictions through *relationships*. Regurgitating Bible facts doesn't make you a godly man. Character is not developed in a lecture hall. Hearing someone expound something eternally fascinating doesn't mean you've forged that information into convictions. There's no guarantee that you'll be more effective for Christ because you study the Bible in-depth. The secret to continuing in the truth is the *relationship* you have with your mentors.

I've had some of the best Bible training in the world. I was privileged to learn God's Word at the highest level from some of the most amazing teachers—some of their names will go down in church history. I thank God every day for the teaching I received. But an alarming number of men who have been exposed to the same teaching no longer believe what they learned. Many of them have defected morally, and some of them don't even believe in God. The problem wasn't with the Bible or the teachers. Rather, it was the backward approach utilized by these students. They are like the "slide climbers" at the playground who go up the slide the wrong way.

As a dad with five kids, I find myself at the park a lot. There's always at least one kid on the playground who wants to get to the top of the jungle gym by going up the slide the wrong way. The "slide climber" won't use the ladder. Instead, he attempts to get to the top another way. If he gets enough of a running start or can position his footing just right, he can finagle his way up the steep six-foot summit. If he is successful, that will allow him to justify his creative approach, but ultimately, he went up the wrong way. He might be able to maintain his balance and even learn to fall safely, but eventually he is going to get a foot in his face from any kid who goes down the slide in the correct manner. It will be even worse if multiple kids go down the slide at the same time. Then they will all come crashing down at the bottom together.

The same is true in the spiritual realm. You can try to climb to the top spiritually in a backward way and deceive yourself into thinking that because you reached the top, your approach is valid. You can reason that you have the skill to go up a different way than what is prescribed and bypass the discipleship ladder altogether. You can convince yourself that because you've never had a serious fall, you are able to slip safely. But just like those "slide climbers" on the playground, one false step and you will crash, sliding down to the bottom, right where you started—humiliated, bruised, and potentially having injured those who followed you. Let's not learn this lesson the hard way. The ideal way to the top is to go up the discipleship ladder, step by step.

Please don't get me wrong. Intense Bible study is totally worth your time. We should all aspire to rightly handle the Scriptures. But put them in their proper context alongside a mentor, and you will have the best combination. Paul taught Timothy the place of truth in his heart, conscience, and faith. He showed Timothy how it influenced his prayers, priorities, and purity. It addressed his weaknesses, insecurities, afflictions, and temptations. There was nothing left untouched by truth.

Paul taught Timothy by imparting information to him in the best context for learning: imitation.

Direction #2: Let Him Model Christ for You

If Paul emphasized anything in his training of Timothy, it's that character is king. Far and away, godliness is infinitely more important than giftedness. As it relates to your spiritual development, your mentor can help you hone the qualities of a man of God. The truth he imparts is meant to change your heart and conduct. Sound doctrine equals sound living. Consider Paul's words to Timothy in the following passage:

> You, however, have followed my teaching, my conduct, my
> aim in life, my faith, my patience, my love, my steadfast-
> ness, my persecutions and sufferings that happened to me

at Antioch, at Iconium, and at Lystra—which persecutions
I endured; yet from them all the Lord rescued me (2 Timothy 3:10-11).

Timothy had seen Paul's conduct up close. He was an eyewitness to how selflessly Paul would spend his life in service for others. He had heard Paul teach and preach on countless occasions. Timothy watched him labor to the point of exhaustion to bring the truth to others. He would have rejoiced with Paul at the conversion of lost sinners. He would have wept with Paul over churches who were seduced by false teaching. He would have learned to pray as he traveled with the apostle. He knew what drove Paul. He had seen Paul beaten, insulted, rejected, ridiculed, and betrayed, only to respond without retaliation. Can't fake that.

For Paul, there was no "Do as I say, not as I do." He supplied the living example of all that he taught. Not that he was perfect, but Paul refused to tolerate hypocrisy in his life. He was conscious of its devastating effects. That's why he took great "pains to have a clear conscience before God and man" (Acts 24:16). That's how he could say with integrity, "Brothers, join in imitating me, and keep your eyes on those who walk according to the example you have in us" (Philippians 3:17).

Timothy was privy to all this. And because Paul had modeled this to Timothy, he knew what to look for in the men he would exalt as the standard in Ephesus.

> The saying is trustworthy: If anyone aspires to the office of overseer, he desires a noble task. Therefore an overseer must be above reproach, the husband of one wife, sober-minded, self-controlled, respectable, hospitable, able to teach, not a drunkard, not violent but gentle, not quarrelsome, not a lover of money. He must manage his own household

well, with all dignity keeping his children submissive, for
if someone does not know how to manage his own house-
hold, how will he care for God's church? (1 Timothy 3:1-5).

Paul insisted that anyone in spiritual leadership "must be above
reproach." That means those who lead should not be guilty of
gross or unrepentant sin in their lives. There's no dirty secret that
would discredit the ministry or besmirch the name of Christ. We
all know examples of leaders who are endowed with amazing abilities but their lifestyle is a wreck. People stop listening to these leaders because their sin gets in the way.

The most important phrase in 1 Timothy 3:1-5 is "must be above
reproach." That's a nonnegotiable. There is to be no lowering of the
standard to accommodate mediocre men. But neither are we to
expect perfection. Being above reproach means living life in a Godward direction so that you become more Christlike. That's the most
important feature of a godly man.

It's also important to realize these qualifications are not limited to
"professional Christians." The call to be above reproach is repeated
for all of us in Philippians 2:15. All of these qualities are commanded
elsewhere for all believers. Leaders aren't held to a higher standard.
Rather, they are more accountable to the *same* standard as the rest
of us (James 3:1).

A prospective mentor must have a track record of godliness if he
is going to lead you. Keep in mind that you are going to have to be
around him often enough and close enough so that you can learn
from him. If he is married, you will want to see how he loves and
serves his wife, and how he reacts when his kids misbehave. You
need to have a vantage point from which to see him under pressure,
when someone wants to draw him into conflict. Your proximity to

him should afford an ongoing view of his work ethic, his spending habits, and what path his eyes take when an attractive woman walks by. Mentoring is modeling, and that can't happen from a distance.

Direction #3: Let Him Fix the Flaws in You

The closer you get to your Paul, the more he is going to see your weaknesses and fatal flaws. Weakness are those areas in which you work from a distinct disadvantage. A fatal flaw is more serious—it is a moral defect that could completely sideline you if left unchecked, and eventually it will ruin you and others. As men, we all have weaknesses and fatal flaws, but we don't like inviting others in to see or fix them. It's embarrassing to have someone poking around and discover the things that shame us—the areas in which we need the most help. We would rather keep other men at a distance. It's safer that way—or so we think.

But if your mentor is going to help you, you're going to have to be authentic. And being authentic requires you to be transparent. Your Paul needs access to you and the freedom to speak into your life. Here are five areas in which Timothy needed Paul's help:

- He felt the pressure of being a young man whose inexperience caused people not to respect him, and he didn't know how to step it up (1 Timothy 4:12).
- He looked too closely at his inadequacies and began to neglect his spiritual gifts (1 Timothy 4:14-16).
- He found it hard to carry the burdens of ministry, which made him physically ill (1 Timothy 5:23).
- He let his fears get to him, which caused him to back away from conflict and problems (2 Timothy 1:7).

- He succumbed to the pressure to be ashamed of Paul, the gospel, and even Jesus Himself (2 Timothy 1:8).

Timothy had inadequacies that he needed to shore up so he could maximize his potential, and his fatal flaws could go so far as to cause him to self-destruct and take out others with him. Inexperience and feelings of inadequacy put him at a disadvantage, and his lack of emotional and physical stamina made it harder to endure harsh treatment. Fear had the potential to take him off mission and give occasion for the enemy to take over and undo everything he and Paul had built. Unwilling to let that happen, Paul moved toward Timothy to help him diffuse his own bomb.

I remember when TSA (Transportation Security Administration) first came out with full-body X-ray scans at airports. At first, everyone understood the need for them in a post-9/11 world. Basic metal detection isn't enough. The security upgrades meant longer lines, but no one wanted to relive that September morning. However, general acceptance turned into a passionate outcry when the public learned the images generated by the full-body scanners were see-all. Virtually nude pictures of every traveler took transparency to a whole new level. Security was now a severe invasion of privacy. It didn't matter that the person viewing the screen was away from the public in a back room—the scanner was too probing.

Today, it's more reasonable. TSA workers see only a somewhat cartoonlike representation of the traveler. If a potentially suspicious object is detected, a bright yellow box appears on the silhouette over the area of concern. Prospective threats are still identified, but travelers retain some sense of privacy (and dignity). It's a more balanced solution for now.

We applaud those who invented the technology that keeps us

safe, and we should feel the same way toward mentors who help keep a watchful eye on us. Everyone is better off when the things that threaten our well-being get removed. Mentoring is not a spiritual see-all, but you do want to allow your mentor to get close enough that he can address any areas of concern in your life. He needs to know the real you. If you hold him at arm's length, he can't help you. You must be honest with him.

One of the most practical things you can do with your Paul is invite and receive his feedback. Evaluation, even when it's highly critical, is the breakfast of champions. We don't grow as well when all people are willing to say is, "Good job...that was great!" Affirmation instills confidence, true enough. But we cannot improve unless we also know the ways in which we are falling short. Get in the habit of asking your mentor questions like these:

- How could I have done that better?
- What do you see that am I missing in this?
- Where do you see me getting distracted from what's most important?
- Is there anything I'm doing that could be a fatal flaw?
- What one thing should I focus on that will make the greatest difference?

Listen to his answers, even if they don't come in the package you like. Work toward solutions and put a plan in place. Let him hold you accountable to that plan. And if you fall, fall forward.

In 2016, American sprinter Jenna Prandini accidentally fell forward yet won her bid to compete in the 200-meter event for the Olympics. In the qualifying race, as Jenna kept pace with her opponents, she lost her footing and staggered, but stayed composed as

A mentor is going to prod you further, drive you harder, and work you longer than you would ever do on your own. **He will push you so as to bring out the best in you.** He will give you a vision for what your life can be, and opportunities to apply what you're learning. Your growth will be measurable.

she fell forward across the finish line. By learning how to fall forward, Jenna advanced to the Olympics by 0.01 of a second. Jenna Prandini didn't intentionally dive to win, but she did illustrate a spiritual reality. You can win even if you fall down in the race. You just have to fall forward.

That's legal in footraces and spiritual races. Having a mentor doesn't guarantee you won't stumble and fall. It means you will have a coach who can tell you how to fall down and still win.

Direction #4: Let Him Entrust Responsibilities to You

Enlisting a Paul is like recruiting a coach—a life trainer. He is going to prod you further, drive you harder, and work you longer than you would ever do on your own. He will push you so as to bring out the best in you. He will give you a vision for what your life can be, and opportunities to apply what you're learning. Your growth will be measurable.

Your Paul is concerned that you see your unique gifts and abilities and know how to exercise them. And he will provide you with a platform to use them for the good of others and the glory of God. The more faithful you are, the more opportunities your mentor will open. He will be happy to stand at the back of the room and shine the spotlight on you.

Bible teacher John MacArthur has compiled a helpful list of responsibilities that Paul gave to Timothy in his letters. Paul expected Timothy to take action and lead in Paul's absence. These responsibilities speak not only of the duties Timothy had, but the confidence Paul had in knowing Timothy would carry them out. Here's a sample from that list, meant to be read slowly.

- Correct those who teach false doctrine and call them to a

pure heart, a good conscience, and a sincere faith (1 Timothy 1:3-5).

- Discipline himself for the purpose of godliness (4:7-11).

- Be gracious and gentle in confronting the sin of his people (5:1-2).

- Guard the Word of God as a sacred trust and a treasure (6:20-21).

In his second epistle, Paul reminded Timothy to do the following:

- Keep the gift of God in him fresh and useful (2 Timothy 1:6).

- Suffer difficulty and persecution willingly, while making the maximum effort for Christ (2:3-7).

- Lead with authority (2:14).

- Interpret and apply Scripture accurately (2:15).

- Not be an arguer but be kind, teachable, gentle, and patient, even when wronged (2:24-26).

- Be sober in all things and endure hardship (4:5).[1]

This is a great list to use as a reference point with your mentor. None of these responsibilities are automatic or downloadable. They require the hard work of discipleship with a mentor. And here's a secret: You don't have to be a pastor to do most of them. Every item on this list is relevant to you in some way, regardless of your station in life.

Was Timothy capable of carrying out this level of responsibility at the beginning? Definitely not. Paul built him up to it. As a wise mentor, he entrusted his disciple with opportunities consistent with his abilities. Then he built from there. He took Timothy from being faithful in little to faithful in much.

When the Driver Becomes the Crew Chief

One of the happiest days in the life of a mentor is the one on which he can *deploy* and *enjoy* his disciple. A discipler is trying to get his disciple to the place where he won't need him anymore. My greatest joy is to see those whom I disciple making wise choices on their own—decisions that set the trajectory for the rest of their lives to continue in a Godward direction. I feel a deep sense of satisfaction when I see them solving life's problems on their own and taking serious ownership of the solutions through to the end. I genuinely love watching them take the initiative to grow independent of me by accumulating knowledge, wisdom, and understanding—truth that will remain when I am gone. I become excited as I watch them form relationships with others whom I know will ultimately replace me—relationships in which there will be stability, accountability, and authenticity. Simply put, a mentor is aware that eventually, he will reach the place at which he knows his disciple has "got it." No one will reach perfection, but every person should strive toward consistent patterns of right thinking and right living.

Timothy went on to reach a place where he didn't need his hand held. I'm sure he would have wanted Paul around forever to answer his questions and critique his decisions, but that was no longer necessary. Timothy was going to cross the finish line just fine. There was nothing else for Paul to impart. Timothy had mastered the track. Sure, there would be other races and racetracks, different turns and terrains. But because of Paul's influence, Timothy would do well.

Better still, Timothy had become skilled to the point that it was his turn to speak into someone else's ear. The driver was becoming a crew chief.

Who is your crew chief? Most men I ask have never had one. I wouldn't take another lap around the track without my crew chief. Once you've found that man, strap on your helmet, make sure your headset is turned on, and push the volume all the way up so that your Paul can help you excel as you navigate your way to the finish line.

Important Takeaways to Remember

- Your success on the track of life is not so much a matter of your ability to handle yourself, but your willingness to pull together a pit crew that keeps you going on well. There is no victory without a pit crew.

- A disciple learns truth, but discipleship is more than simply acquiring Bible knowledge. You don't know it until you do it.

- The key to maintaining your convictions is remembering those who imparted them to you. The secret to continuing in those convictions is the relationships you've had with your mentors.

- One of the best ways to learn is through imitation. Find a godly man whose example you can follow. Mentoring is modeling, and that can't happen from a distance.

- A weakness is an area at which you work from a distinct disadvantage. A fatal flaw is a moral defect that could completely sideline you and ruin you and others if left unchecked.

- For guys, the most common fatal flaws are gold, glory, and girls.

- Growth doesn't mean you don't fall down. You can win even if you fall. You just have to fall forward.

- Feedback is vital to spiritual growth. You cannot improve unless you know the ways in which you are falling short. Invite and receive input, even if it doesn't come in the package you like.

- There is a right way and a wrong way to approach godliness. It's tempting to try to get to the top faster by going backward, but you will not avoid slipping and falling. Use the discipleship ladder.

Finding Your Paul

In the relationship between Paul and Timothy, it was Paul who initiated the connection. Timothy was willing and available. That doesn't mean you have to wait around for someone to ask to mentor you—you could be waiting a long time. If you don't have a mentor, find one. But just as race car drivers should be selective in their choice of a crew chief, so should you make sure you find the right mentor. Here are some things you can do now to get started:

1. Paul spotted Timothy as someone whom he wanted to disciple because Timothy was already growing in his walk. Timothy had the potential that would make mentoring a worthwhile investment for Paul. As you think about your spiritual growth, what can you point to that would catch the eye of a crew chief? Why would someone want to mentor you? Write down what you see, and why you would be up for the challenge.

2. This chapter discussed how a mentor helps you shore up weaknesses and fix fatal flaws. Be honest with yourself and identify any shortcomings that could hinder you from reaching your full potential in Christ. Are any of them fatal flaws?

These need the attention of a mentor. Make a list of your top three potential fatal flaws. As you do so, consider the ones listed in this chapter: gold, glory, and girls. Which of your flaws has the strongest pull on you, and what do you need to do to overcome that pull?

3. Titus 2 describes discipling relationships among men in the context of a high-impact church ministry. Read that chapter and write down what you learn about how men should help other men grow, and what the outcome ought to be. List the qualities of a godly mentor and a growing disciple:

4. Review John MacArthur's partial list of duties that Paul gave Timothy to perform. You do not need to be a pastor to carry out these responsibilities. Go back and circle the three items

in the list that you think would make the most difference in your life if a mentor were to model them for you. Then start looking for someone who excels in these areas and ask him if he would be willing to teach you how he does those things. Do the names of any prospective mentors come to mind right now?

CHAPTER 2

You Need a Solid Peer to Encourage You

This year, thousands of men will die from stubbornness." I was driving when I saw this line plastered on a billboard. It caught my attention and forced me to do a double take. *Really? I didn't know stubbornness was fatal.*

It took me a few seconds to realize what the advertisers were going for—men don't usually seek help until it's too late. The ad was a plea for men to get regular medical checkups. A prompt to let someone else look under the hood and do some diagnostics. Most men apparently don't, and the results are catastrophic. We die not because we have problems that can't be treated; we die because we're stubborn.

Men are tough by design, but toughness can be fatal if it becomes stubbornness that causes us to slide into a false sense of security and refuse to ask for help. We don't want someone else to slow us down, and we don't like to stop and ask for directions. We want others to need us. And that's not all wrong. God wired us with a strong sense of independence, but when we fail to see the value of involving other men in our lives, we suffer needlessly.

Of all the friends we might have, the Bible urges us to seek the kinds of men who will walk alongside us and leave us better off than when they found us. This is what the apostle Paul had in Barnabas, a spiritual peer who encouraged him. Barnabas is one of the best examples in all of Scripture of what it means to be a treasured and inspiring friend. Because of his relationship with Paul, he has touched millions of people throughout history.

We are introduced to Barnabas in Acts 4, just as the early church had begun to experience its first wave of persecution. Despite threats and beatings, early believers were unmoved in their commitment to the Lord. That was true, in large measure, because of men like Barnabas, who were leading, serving, encouraging, and sustaining the flock of God.

Barnabas's given name was Joseph, but the apostles called him Barnabas, which means "son of encouragement" (Acts 4:36). That was his nickname because that was his character. The name *Barnabas* refers to someone who exhorts and comforts. He's a come-alongside, a helper. He's a backup. Someone who stands in the gap. A wingman. He's the kind of man who gets into your life for your upbuilding, and he does it in ways that bring immediate benefits. When he's with you, you're recharged and motivated.

But he's not like your dog, tongue out and tail wagging when you walk through the door, ready to play catch. He can say the hard things too. If he has to make wounds, he will, but he also knows how to heal them. If he has to rebuke you, he isn't afraid of hurting your feelings, but he also knows how to give you hope. If you are struggling, he knows how to motivate you to keep going and not give up. He isn't heavy-handed, but he's also not light on sin. He maintains a good balance.

In your personal pit crew, Barnabas functions like your tire changer. He comes alongside you to replace your treads when you are wearing thin or cracking. He's attentive to the pressure on your inside and the durability on your outside. He knows how to spot embedded debris and detect the warble of wheels out of balance. With precision and speed, your tire changer keeps you on track so that you will have a sure grip as you progress toward the finish line. This is the kind of guy you want around.

How to Know When You Need New Tires

Barnabas was indispensable to Paul. There were five critical times in Paul's life when that friendship would matter most, when Paul needed Barnabas's torque wrench. When we study those events, we discover the marks of the kind of peer you need in your life, someone who is at your same station in life spiritually. Here they are:

Mark #1: A Barnabas Takes Risks on You When Others Reject You

Before Paul became a believer, he was hostile to Christians, killing them as fast as he could. Anything to stop the Jesus movement. Next to Satan, he was the worst villain of Christianity until he came face to face with the risen Lord Jesus. That day, Paul was exposed to the horrifying reality that everything he knew and believed was a lie. He had been wrong about everything. Earth-shattering.

But now, Paul was alive in Christ. He had been forgiven by the Lord whom he was attacking. As hateful as he had been, he became just as bold for Christ. He preached with such passion that he became public enemy number one. As a result, he was forced to flee for his life to the place where he was sure he would find welcome—Jerusalem. Or so he thought. He was a marked man there too.

Paul's past followed him. His reputation haunted him. No one trusted him. They assumed it was a trap. The risk wasn't worth it. He was a man without a country. The Jewish leaders hated him, and the church was afraid of him. No one wanted anything to do with him. He was in a difficult and dangerous place: a brand-new Christian, totally alone. He was a spiritual infant left on the doorstep of the church, and they weren't answering the doorbell. Insert Barnabas.

Here is the value of this kind of friend: *He believes the best about what God can do in your life.* Barnabas listened to Paul's story, heard the testimony of his transformed life, inspected the claims to see if his words were true, then took him before the apostles and argued his case for him. In and through his encouragement, Barnabas overcame their fears. Barnabas put himself on the line for Paul.

That's what a biblical friend like Barnabas does. He chooses to trust you, take risks on you, believe the best about you, and always give you the benefit of the doubt. He takes the time to know you at a deeper level, where who you are and what you have done doesn't push him away from you. He's the kind of man to whom you can open up and be honest. You can tell him anything, and he won't rub your nose in it. A Barnabas believes God is big enough to produce real change in you. He sees your potential and steps toward you with whatever you need to keep going.

The result of the risk Barnabas took on Paul is recorded for us:

> He [Paul] was with them, moving about freely in Jerusalem, speaking out boldly in the name of the Lord. And he was talking and arguing with the Hellenistic Jews; but they were attempting to put him to death. But when the

A Barnabas chooses to trust you, take risks on you, believe the best about you, and always give you the benefit of the doubt… **He believes God is big enough to produce real change in you.** He sees your potential and steps toward you with whatever you need to keep going.

brethren learned of it, they brought him down to Caesarea
and sent him away to Tarsus (Acts 9:28-30 NASB).

Barnabas's encouragement gave Paul a platform for ministry and
a boldness for the gospel. But more boldness meant more persecution. Paul was so hated he had to flee again. This was a good thing.
He was a standout thanks to God's work through a friend.

Mark #2: A Barnabas Serves Alongside You When Opportunities Open

For the next decade and a half, God took Paul out of play to prepare him for the ministry he would have. Meanwhile, He used others to press the frontier of the gospel forward. Then in Acts 11, the
apostles learned that Jews from Cyprus were preaching the gospel
and that God was at work. So they sent Barnabas to check things out
and report back. It was his hometown. He was the obvious choice.

But once Barnabas got there and saw God moving, he "began to
encourage them all with resolute heart to remain true to the Lord"
(verse 23 NASB). Of course he did. That's what encouragers do. They
make you stronger, firmer, and more resolute. Wherever he was, this
was his manner because this was his life.

While Barnabas was there, he remembered the guy who had
been set apart as "the apostle to the Gentiles" 14 years ago. So he
left that work to find Paul. This was Paul's moment, and Barnabas
wanted to make sure he didn't miss it. After searching for Paul, Barnabas found him and helped him get the start he needed in ministry. Over the course of the next year they labored together shoulder
to shoulder.

This is instructive. An encourager doesn't lead alone. He's no
Marlboro man. He doesn't think the world revolves around him.
He thrives best in spiritual partnership. A Barnabas wants you to be

what God created you to be and provides the opportunity for you to use your abilities. He sees what God has put into you and is zealous that you serve the Lord to full capacity. It might mean he has to give up some of the limelight. So what! No ego here.

Encouragers find their greatest joy when you thrive. If you are going to excel, you need someone who recognizes the work of Christ in you and can match you with the right role. He finds great joy in sharing the privileges with you, and doesn't feel like he has to micromanage you. He sees that your gifts make room for you, even before you see how.

As a boy, did you ever shoot hoops on the blacktop and imagine yourself in the championship game? In your mind, your team is down by two, and you get the ball with five seconds left on the clock—it's you and one defender. As you plant at the three-point line, you can see the red numbers in slow motion: *THREE… TWO…* (ball releases) *ONE…* (BUZZER) and *swish*, nothing but net! The crowd goes wild. Not Barnabas. He's got the ball with five seconds left on a breakaway. He charges to the net, feet leaving the floor. But instead of jamming it in, he sees you open…he passes! You are on the side, no defender, your feet firmly planted at the three-point line. You can see the red numbers in slow motion: *THREE… TWO…* (ball releases) *ONE…* (BUZZER) and *swish*, nothing but net! The crowd goes wild.

Barnabas wants *you* to make the shot. If he believes you have the best angle, you're getting the ball. It's about a win for the Lord, not his own highlight reel. This is how a Barnabas thinks. And for a season, these men developed a strong tag-team relationship. This would prime them for what God wanted them to do next: their first missionary journey.

In Acts 13, we read that once Paul and Barnabas finished the work in Cyprus, they continued on in Antioch. Luke records, "While they were ministering to the Lord and fasting, the Holy Spirit said, 'Set apart for Me Barnabas and Saul [Paul] for the work to which I have called them.' Then, when they had fasted and prayed and laid their hands on them, they sent them away" (verses 1-3 NASB).

Notice how God calls—it's when we are already in motion, active and engaged in service. He doesn't want us sitting idle, waiting for someone to discover us. God wants us to be willing to do the work without a title, without recognition. Wherever we are, that is the most important assignment. Whoever we are talking to, that's the most important person in our world.

When you see this in a man, you've found a Barnabas. Join him. Find a way to serve with him in any opportunity that arises, whether behind the scenes or on the front lines. Shadow him. See if you can help him, even in the menial things. Learn from him. Then when God is ready to unleash you to lead, you'll be ready and equipped. What happened in the early church will happen to you and your Barnabas—God will send out His best.

By contrast, beware of guys who are good at posturing. You know who I'm talking about: ego-centered manipulators. Some are more obvious than others. These guys use their connections to advance themselves. They play spiritual favorites and drop names. They are territorial. They don't share, or if they do, while they may lend a hand, it's clear you need them, but they don't need you. You are favorable to them so long as you remember your place. These guys are climbers.

Guys like this can't seem to affirm God at work in others. They want to be the one in charge and, ironically enough, they are thin-skinned and hate criticism. But because they have passion, people follow them. It's stunning how addicting these men are and how often they get exalted. Here's my advice: Don't be that guy. And when you see one, run away.

You have unique gifts and abilities that only you can use. God also has a specific ministry for you. A Barnabas will draw that out of you and make room for you. This is the kind of scenario God uses to turn the world upside down. Where would Paul have been if Barnabas had not made room for God's call on his life? The New Testament would read quite differently.

Mark #3: A Barnabas Remains Steadfast by You When Opposition Arises

Throughout that missionary journey, Paul and Barnabas experienced many highs and lows. The greater their success, the crueler the opposition they faced. But they were able to keep moving onward because of their mutual encouragement to each other. They also helped each other to stand against compromise.

On one occasion, a superstitious crowd mistook Paul and Barnabas for the mythical gods Hermes and Zeus. The people saw the power of God on display in the two men and decided to worship them. This left Paul and Barnabas in shock and horror. Lesser men probably would have used this platform to gain an audience and further their cause. Instead, Paul and Barnabas had a single-minded passion for God's glory that drove the crowd to quell it.

That is how you recognize a Barnabas: He doesn't touch the glory. He doesn't let you touch it either. Paul and Barnabas "rushed out into the crowd, crying out and saying, 'Men, why are you doing these things? We are also men of the same nature as you, and preach the gospel to you that you should turn from these vain things to a living God, who made the heaven and the earth and the sea and all that is in them'" (Acts 14:14-15). Just as these two were trying to convince the people that they weren't gods, they got some help. But not the kind of help they expected:

> Jews came from Antioch and Iconium, and having won over the crowds, they stoned Paul and dragged him out of the city, supposing him to be dead. But while the disciples stood around him, he got up and entered the city. The next day he went away with Barnabas to Derbe (Acts 14:19-20).

Just as if he were on Facebook, Paul had followers. But they weren't a fan club. They were haters. Still angry about what Paul and Barnabas had stirred up in the previous city, they decided to end Paul's life by stoning him. Stoning is not a pleasant experience, from what I can tell. First the crowd mobs you and pummels you. Then they take you to the edge of the city and throw you off a small cliff (if one is available). The fall is meant to disable you so that you remain still while the crowd pelts you with rocks up to the size of volleyballs. Instant grave. No need for a burial. You just got one.

This mob wouldn't settle for intimidating the apostle. They wanted to make sure that he was dead. But Paul was immortal until God's work for him was done. Somehow he managed to crawl out from under the rocks, dust himself off, go back into the city, and finish his sermon. I love it. Nothing stops the gospel! That's Paul. That's his Savior.

And who was there with Paul to cheer, strengthen, and embolden him? It was his wingman, Barnabas. In praise and pain, Barnabas stood by Paul so that he could remain faithful. When the going got tough, Barnabas kept Paul going.

The impact of a Barnabas cannot be overstated. In times of testing, true encouragers help you remain uncompromising. They remind you to stay humble in success as well as faithful in hardship.

They pick you up when you fall down, and dust you off and send you back into the fray—and they come with you. They never leave you. They are in it for the duration. Together you can prompt each other to lie low and exalt Christ. You can draw strength from each other.

I have a few men like this in my life—some of them in ministry with me, and some on speed dial. They know me. They give me feedback. They know my gifts and abilities and support me in them. They are also aware of my tendencies toward sin, and stand in my way. They know where I am weak, and put their shoulder under the load to help me carry it. They can sense my discouragement, and know just how to point me back to Christ. They are the kind of men I can trust because I know they have my back. Every man needs someone like that.

Mark #4: A Barnabas Clashes with You When Convictions Collide

Paul and Barnabas were fiercely loyal to each other, and that forged a strong bond. You might consider them a "dream team." This dynamic duo passionately fought almost every kind of battle on every kind of front. Whatever the situation, they were there for each other. Everyone benefited, and we've already seen why.

But one day, their loyalty faced its most serious test. Luke described the incident as a "sharp disagreement" (Acts 15:39). The issue was John Mark, who "had deserted them" (verse 38). If you go back and read the story in Acts 13, you learn when the work of ministry became too heavy, John Mark abandoned them.

This was no small matter because the word "deserted" is not a favorable term. It means "to forsake, withdraw, or revolt." In military language, it means to go AWOL in a time of war. This departure was so strong that Luke used a Greek word that also describes a person who denies the faith. It seems things fell apart when John Mark heard Paul going toe-to-toe with a false teacher. That guy was talking people out of believing the gospel, and apparently it rattled John Mark too. It appears that he came just short of denying his own faith. He bailed, and Paul and Barnabas had to go on without him.

Back home, it looks like John Mark got his act together and his name came up again. Paul wanted to go back and visit the cities where they had ministered, and Barnabas wanted to give John Mark a second chance. That's what a Barnabas does, after all—he believes the best, takes risks, and trusts when no one else will.

By contrast, "Paul kept insisting that they should *not* take him along" (verse 38). They clashed hard. Neither of them budged. They were at an impasse. So "they separated from one another, and Barnabas took Mark with him and sailed away to Cyprus" (verse 39). This is hard to reconcile, given all they had been through together. In one sense, it's encouraging to know that no less than Paul and Barnabas had issues. Even godly men sometimes close the door, raise their voices, and disagree with passion. That's not all bad. Each man had his own preference, and for good reason each stood firm on his convictions. But it took their 17-year-old friendship to the melting point.

You can understand both sides, right?

Paul would have held a firm "No!" because John Mark left them high and dry when he deserted them. He would truly have to prove himself before he could be trusted again. The risk was too great. Added to that were these nagging fears: What if it happened again? What if there was another conflict and John Mark couldn't get away like before? What if the pressure was too great and he denied Christ? That would not be good for the mission or the man.

Barnabas, the encourager he was, saw the best in John Mark and his ability to learn from his mistakes. He saw John shaken up, and he must have seen that John had gotten his issues all sorted out. It's true that taking John Mark again was a risk, but that's what a Barnabas does—he takes risks on people. He could have reminded Paul about the time when no one was willing to take a risk on him. Not even the apostles believed he was a changed man. Paul had done some pretty awful things—in fact, they were much worse. Where would he be if Barnabas had treated Paul like Paul was treating John? Barnabas could have read some of Paul's letters back to him about grace, mercy, and forgiveness. John deserved a second chance.

Who was right? Both men stood convinced; both men refused to budge. Strong leaders are strong. Now what? Barnabas decided to take John Mark to Cyprus, and Paul picked another ministry partner.

In God's providence, this was a good idea, for several reasons. Cyprus was the exact point of departure where John Mark had gone AWOL before. Maybe Barnabas wanted to take him back and work on what had gone wrong so he could strengthen him. Cyprus was also Barnabas's hometown. He knew it well. He could mentor John Mark in a low-impact way. He could nurture John to the point where he would prove himself faithful.

Paul, on the other hand, could leave and push the frontier of the gospel forward as God had called him to do. He could even travel into hostile territory without the distraction of hand-holding. He could minister freely. Instead of one missionary team, there were now two. Both of them went their separate ways. Both Paul and Barnabas could fulfill their passions without compromising their convictions. The kingdom benefited because the work of Christ could continue to flourish. Paul and Barnabas were effective both apart and together.

In our relationships with other men, if we live with conviction, we will eventually collide. It's inevitable, even in men who love the Lord. We won't back down. We won't always agree. In fact, some of our disagreements will be sharp. Sometimes we will part ways after some of the sweetest memories together. That's not the ideal, but it can happen. Even so, God can use those kinds of situations to sharpen us. That's what Proverbs 27:17 means when it says, "Iron sharpens iron, so one man sharpens another." Iron only sharpens iron when it clashes, and sometimes that is unavoidable in relationships.

Having an encourager doesn't mean that your Barnabas will roll over and defer to you. Godly men don't use rubber stamps. A Barnabas will push back on you. He will not compromise his convictions, but neither will he become bitter. He is more loyal to the Lord than to you. Yet loyal he remains.

Mark #5: A Barnabas Stays Loyal to You When Paths Diverge

At this point in Bible history, Barnabas virtually vanishes. He's done in Acts. The Bible makes a couple more passing references to him, but those references tell us little. The irony is that the remainder of what we know about Barnabas comes from the pen of Paul himself. And it speaks of their enduring loyalty to each other.

In 1 Corinthians 9, Paul had to defend his integrity against accusations that he was in ministry to get rich. The allegations made no sense. It's interesting to note that as Paul argued for his own rights in the gospel, he went a step further to defend Barnabas. Barnabas wasn't even in the conversation. He was ministering elsewhere with John Mark, the former deserter. Despite their unresolved disagreement, Paul defended the integrity and ministry of Barnabas. He still valued Barnabas's proven worth. When Paul spoke of him, he spoke well. He protected his brother's reputation. Barnabas didn't even know what Paul was doing. It takes a real man to do this.

The lesson is this: Conflict should not diminish our loyalty to one another. We may fight *with* our Barnabas, but we should also fight *for* our Barnabas, even behind his back. We should never throw him under the bus.

The only other reference to Barnabas, which portrays his loyalty best of all, is found in Paul's final epistle written at the end of his life, 2 Timothy. Paul, knowing that he would soon be martyred for the faith, asked to be joined in prison by the one man that Barnabas had spent the rest of his days mentoring: "Pick up Mark and bring him with you, for he is useful to me for service" (2 Timothy 4:11). Of all the people Paul could have wanted with him during his final days, he asked for John Mark. I've sat on the floor of the Mamertine prison in Rome, where Paul wrote those words. It's a dark, dingy, humid, claustrophobic underground cave. Prisoners had to be lowered down into the dungeon by a rope through a small hole about the size of a toilet seat. They would be kept there for months at a time. No bathrooms. An underwater spring often bubbled up and left the prisoners standing knee-deep in water. The Romans would pack about 50 men in there at a time. Imagine Paul standing knee-deep in refuse, writing his last will and testament. Who does he want? Barnabas's protege.

At one point, Paul refused to use John Mark in his ministry. Paul lost his best ministry partner over him. This turncoat, this mama's boy, this "can't take the heat so he's getting out of the kitchen" coward had abandoned them when they needed him most. But now the apostle asked for John Mark by name because he was useful.

How did John Mark move from useless to useful? As far as we can tell, Barnabas spent the rest of his life discipling John Mark. He expended his last days behind the scenes, quietly investing in a man who was where Paul was when Barnabas first found him. The cycle was repeating, to the glory of God. John Mark had needed a Barnabas to take a risk on him. It had been years since Paul had last seen Barnabas. Their last memory of each other had been incredibly painful. But Paul was affirming how powerfully influential Barnabas had been on his life.

Impact that Outlasts Friendship

Barnabas's influence through John Mark remains to this day in another powerful way. Have you ever read the Gospel of Mark? That's *John* Mark, the same guy! The one who got close enough to the edge of apostasy that he almost fell off the cliff. The same man who wasn't worth the risk to Paul. God used that guy to write sacred Scripture. Through Barnabas's leadership and mentoring, Mark got it. Barnabas had replicated and replaced himself.

If you have ever read the second book of the New Testament and drawn closer to Christ, you have been changed by Barnabas. If you have ever studied the letters of Paul and come into a purer devotion to Christ, you owe an immeasurable debt of thanks to the "son of encouragement." Barnabas shows us how to leave an impact that outlasts a friendship.

Do you have a guy like Barnabas in your life? He's not a mentor or a disciple, but a spiritual peer who helps you spot a slow leak and prevent a blowout. Every race-car driver knows how vital all four tires are at every turn, and how there is never a time we can risk bypassing the pit to shave a few seconds off the clock.

· · · · · · · · · · · · · ·

Pixar's movie *Cars* made this point in its first animated film. An overconfident Lightning McQueen was too happy with himself to believe he could lose, so rather than taking advice from his pit crew, he exasperated them until nearly everyone quit. During the race, his remaining crew members repeatedly urged him to pull into the pit for new tires, and just like we do sometimes, he became so transfixed on winning that he minimized the need for anything but gas. Rounding the final turn of the last lap with a strong lead in first place, McQueen predictably and foolishly lost each one of his tires. Fishtailing on his rims and sending fiery sparks into the air, the desperate racer twisted and clawed his way toward the finish line. With the other cars bearing down on him, Lightning McQueen lunged forward and stuck out his tongue just in time for a photo-finish tie for first.

Needlessly, that's how we look when we are stubborn, self-reliant, and whiz past our Barnabas. As tempted as you might be to finish the race without your tire man because you are so fixed on the finish line, don't. Even if you don't think your rubber is wearing thin, it's not worth the risk. Pull over. Let your brothers in Christ stretch, challenge, and help you. Don't suffer because of stubbornness. Seek, find, and be a Barnabas.

Important Takeaways to Remember

- Men are tough by design, but toughness can be fatal if it becomes stubbornness.

- A true friend believes the best about what God can do in your life, even if you seemed unredeemable at one time.

- A Barnabas wants you to be what God created you to be and provides the opportunity for you to use your abilities. He is zealous that you serve the Lord to full capacity.

- Barnabas wants *you* to make the shot. If he believes you have the best angle, you're getting the ball. It's about a win for the Lord, not his own highlight reel.

- A Barnabas doesn't touch the glory. He doesn't let you touch it either. Together, you prompt each other to lie low and exalt Christ.

- In our relationships with other men, if we live with conviction, eventually we will collide. It's inevitable, even in men who love the Lord. It's not the ideal, but iron sharpens iron only when they clash.

- A Barnabas will not compromise his convictions, but neither will he become bitter. He is more loyal to the Lord than to you, yet loyal he remains.

- Conflict should not diminish our loyalty to one another. We may fight *with* our Barnabas, but we should also fight *for* our Barnabas, even behind his back.

- As tempted as you might be to finish the race without your tire man because you are so fixed on the finish line, don't.

Finding Your Barnabas

Everyone needs a Barnabas. He is a nurturer who can see the big picture even when you can't. He will cast and recast the biblical vision to keep you motivated when you might be tempted to quit or do something foolish. He unites and inspires. He's a safe place where you can turn because he won't abuse your friendship to force you into serving his agenda. Instead, he will push you to keep God's agenda and go at God's pace. The following questions will help you discover, develop, and deepen that relationship.

1. Write down a list of names of men who are at or about the same level of spiritual maturity as you. Briefly note which guys possess the qualities of a spiritual encourager. Circle three of the names who have the most likeness to Barnabas. These are the men in your life whom you need to spend time with, even if they don't live near you.

2. Take a short personal inventory of your heart. Where is the tread on your spiritual tires balding or cracking right now? And what's causing that? Are you grappling with guilt, fear, anger, or despair? A Barnabas will protect and cover you, but

he will also challenge you. Is one of the men on your list above a safe enough "place" for you to confide your struggle?

3. What is your conflict strategy? Do you become an intimidator who pushes back and forces your way? Are you the guy who pulls away and pouts, manipulating until you get your way? Do you become high-minded and critical because your ideas and insights aren't valued? Or do you go silent and stand aloof in judgment of those whom you disagree with? Describe how you tend to respond to conflict, and how a Barnabas could keep you focused on kingdom priorities in the midst of conflict.

4. Can you think of any man in your life whom you once considered to be a dear friend, but the relationship is now severely

strained? Maybe you two have had your own sharp disagreement and have decided to go your own separate ways. How have you handled that person's reputation since then—in your thoughts, words, and deeds? Is there anything in place that could help move you back toward righteous closure? Do you need to reach out and make the first move? It's always the right time, and it's always your turn. Do it now.

CHAPTER 3

You Need a Best Friend to Uphold You

No one wants to be alone. Guys who pretend they do don't. It's not even manly. We were made for relationships—with God and others. It's part of being His image bearer. Think about it. It's difficult to walk the Christian life on our own. The greatest commandments, to love God and others, demand ongoing, proactive relationships (Matthew 22:34-40). And relationships require time together. In fact, 56 times in the New Testament we are given commands that relate to "one another." We cannot obey these scriptures if we isolate ourselves.

Think about the flip side: We do stupid things when we are alone. We get careless and shortsighted and make dumb decisions (see Proverbs 24:6). We become inward focused and get out of reach. "Whoever isolates himself seeks his own desire; he breaks out against all sound judgment" (Proverbs 18:1).

When the Best of Men Are at Their Worst

We make ourselves vulnerable when we are alone. That's why Satan sought to tempt Jesus when He was isolated in the wilderness (Matthew 4:1-11). Without others around us, we have a higher failure rate. In Jesus's case it didn't work, but it often does in ours and in men better than us. Ask Elijah, David, and John the Baptist. They show us that even the best of men are at their worst when they are all alone.

When Elijah was by himself in the desert, he became despondent and suicidal. He ran a few ultramarathons in just a couple of days to hide from a woman who threatened his life. He lost perspective, stepped away from his ministry, and begged to die. This from one of the most powerful prophets in the Old Testament!

When David was alone on his roof and saw a woman bathing on a nearby rooftop, he raged inside with sexual lust. He took a trusted friend's girl and tried to cover up his adultery with deception and murder. Yet here is a guy whom God said was "a man after his own heart" (1 Samuel 13:14).

When John the Baptist was alone in prison, he struggled with doubts over whether Jesus was the Messiah. He questioned Jesus's identity, life purpose, mission, and ministry. That, in turn, unraveled everything he believed about his own identity, life purpose, mission, and ministry. But Jesus said John the Baptist was the greatest man who ever lived (Luke 7:28). Strong men struggle too, especially when they are alone.

In each of these cases, God provided friends. Elisha came alongside Elijah to carry his mantle. Nathan lovingly rebuked David to get him back on the path to purity. John's disciples came back from Jesus with a few verses from Isaiah that confirmed Jesus was indeed the long-awaited Messiah.

Having the right friends is essential to your spiritual health as a follower of Jesus. **If you want to see what direction your life is taking and where you will end up, look at the guys who influence you.** That's what you are and are becoming.

We're talking here about some of the stronger men in the Bible—stronger than you or me. And they needed friends. Solomon, the wisest man to ever live, said it well in Ecclesiastes 4:9-12:

> Two are better than one, because they have a good reward for their toil. For if they fall, one will lift up his fellow. But woe to him who is alone when he falls and has not another to lift him up! Again, if two lie together, they keep warm, but how can one keep warm alone? And though a man might prevail against one who is alone, two will withstand him—a threefold cord is not quickly broken.

You need friends. They have the power to make or break you. Certain types of friends are dangerous (Proverbs 1:10-33). Let the wrong guys into your life, and that will lead to your undoing. Proverbs 13:20 declares, "Whoever walks with the wise becomes wise, but the companion of fools will suffer harm." James 4:4 says, "Do you not know that friendship with the world is enmity with God? Therefore whoever wishes to be a friend of the world makes himself an enemy of God."

Having the right friends is essential to your spiritual health as a follower of Jesus. If you want to see what direction your life is taking and where you will end up, look at the guys who influence you. That's what you are and are becoming.

The Definition of a True Friend

What is a friend? In the Old Testament, it's someone who joins you on a journey as both companion and guide. He is a man you can trust, respect, and enjoy along the way. The New Testament pushes the definition further by adding affection, closeness, and partnership. True friends uphold one another with love and loyalty.

If ever there was such a relationship, it's the one modeled for us by David and his best friend Jonathan. Their story appears in 1 Samuel. Their friendship is the gold standard of what true brotherhood should look like among men who are passionate for God. Jonathan is the kind of guy whom every Christian man needs. It's through this kind of friend that God helps you become "a man after his own heart" (1 Samuel 13:14).

The day David and Jonathan met, Israel was at war with their archnemesis, the Philistines. Jonathan, the king's son, had been leading the charge for his father, Saul. With confidence in God's power and jealousy for God's glory, Jonathan put the opposing army to flight. He was a man who fought for God, loved God, and wanted more than anything to be used of God to defeat His enemies. He possessed all the necessary leadership qualities to be the next king.

Everything was going well until the Philistines unveiled their secret weapon. They had a nine-foot-tall giant named Goliath, a foreboding villain. As Darth Vader was to the Galactic Empire or Sauron to Middle Earth, so Goliath was to Israel. He struck fear in everyone and issued a challenge for Israel that the army didn't know how to answer:

> He stood and shouted to the ranks of Israel, "Why have you come out to draw up for battle? Am I not a Philistine, and are you not servants of Saul? Choose a man for yourselves, and let him come down to me. If he is able to fight with me and kill me, then we will be your servants. But if I prevail against him and kill him, then you shall be our servants and serve us." And the Philistine said, "I defy the ranks of Israel this day. Give me a man, that we may fight together." When Saul and all Israel heard these words of the

Philistine, they were dismayed and greatly afraid (1 Samuel 17:8-11).

Goliath was suggesting something called representative battle. Each side picked their best warrior, and the two would fight. The losing side would surrender themselves and become slaves of the winning side. No one ever actually surrendered like that, best we can tell historically. Armies used this strategy more to provoke the battle by giving it a starting point.

Goliath's intimidation was so strong that his challenge went unanswered for 40 days. Twice a day, he came out and taunted Israel. Do the math. That's 80 times that God's army was so scared they became a parade of Disney princesses. Not a single soldier in the army of God's people was even willing to try. It's sad when strong men live in defeat.

This day, however, was not like the last 40. David showed up. The shepherd boy came to the battlefront on an errand. He just happened to show up in the middle of Goliath's rant. He was there to deliver cheese for his brothers (1 Samuel 17:18)—he hadn't planned on joining the fight and didn't know anything about Goliath. But he stood there in holy horror as he heard the slander of his God spewed out like venom. David experienced the shame of seeing his own army run away faster than a scalded dog.

Seeing nothing but embarrassment and resentment in the eyes of the king and soldiers, the boy with no chest hair stepped up. David burst into the situation room with a zeal that could not be contained. He offered himself to the man who should have volunteered to fight Goliath—King Saul, who was the tallest man in Israel, head and shoulders above any other man. But Saul was afraid because he knew that God had rejected him. This could be his end.

You know the story. David went to a brook, where he found five stones that had been made smooth by water. Into a pouch they went. The boy then stepped onto the open field, carrying only his slingshot. The field sloped on both sides with a wide plateau in between, which only Goliath occupied. Both cheers and jeers filled the air.

Those who blinked missed it. A rock that was probably a bit larger than a golf ball flew from David's sling and sunk into the giant's forehead. The noise on both sides stopped completely. David's breathing could be heard as he ran toward the man who was dead when he hit the grass. At the flash of a sword larger than David's body, Goliath's head was dangling in the air. *Four stones left. Got any more giants?*

As the Philistines retreated, David held up his trophy by a fistful of hair. As he walked into the presence of the relieved king, we read that "the soul of Jonathan was knit to the soul of David" (18:1). This is astounding: Jonathan became David's best friend *before* they met. How does that happen? Don't you have to know someone before you become his friend, let alone his best friend? What drew them together? What was the foundation of their friendship? The answer tells us everything we need to know about biblical friendships: The key to their closeness was the glory of God.

The Qualities of Biblical Friendships

All biblical friendships are rooted in a mutual desire to see God glorified. Your best friend will be someone who wants God on display before all people and above all things. Because that was already in place, David and Jonathan had the makings of an ideal friendship. As we follow their story, we learn that some of the best friends we could ever have will evidence these four qualities.

Quality #1: Conviction

Scripture says Jonathan was "knit" to David. The word means "to be tightly and inseparably bound together," like a knot. This kind of relationship can't happen through finding common interests like cars, sports, hunting, or music. Those things aren't wrong, but spiritual friendships go deeper. They include an attachment in the "soul"—a sacred bond.

Jonathan and David were drawn together because of their deep-seated conviction about God's worth. Jonathan saw David summon power to his soul to act because David could not stand by as God was dishonored by Goliath. His rock-hard beliefs about giving all honor and glory to God compelled him to live with courage and godliness.

The biblical concept of God's glory refers to His heaviness and weightiness. Who God is matters. He is significant, awesome, majestic, beautiful, and worthy. Everything about Him—His power, love, sovereignty, knowledge, wisdom, grace, mercy, kindness, goodness, justice, patience, righteousness, faithfulness, unchangeableness, wrath, self-sufficiency, and holiness—has a profound effect on us. Or at least they should.

Each of God's perfections is powerfully motivating. They make us want to know, desire, love, trust, worship, walk with, wait on, obey, enjoy, and serve Him. It's heart, soul, mind, and strength bent toward God with everything full throttle. It's a consuming desire to spend all our lives for Him. John Piper is known for the expression "Going hard after the holy God."[2] That's what David did. That's what Jonathan saw, and that's also what Jonathan was.

Unlike his dad, Jonathan had the same passionate convictions in his heart as David. In the raid on the Philistines earlier in 1 Samuel, Jonathan's convictions about God caused him to speak and act with the exact same confidence as David had shown against Goliath (1 Samuel 14:6). Same heart. Same God. Same bold strength.

Jonathan's soul was knit to David because they *both* lived with a passion for God. This was true before they met. Their likeminded convictions brought them together and kept them together. Psalm 119:63 describes this kind of kindred friendship: "I am a companion of all who fear you, of those who keep your precepts." That's the kind of friend you are looking for and should aspire to be.

In friendships, there is a principle that rings true: *like attracts like*. Godly people will attract godly people; and ungodly people will attract ungodly people. Stop for a minute and think about your closest guy friends. What kinds of men are you drawn most to, and who is most drawn to you? What is the nature of those friendships? Read through your latest text threads. Let your mind drift back to your conversations. Can you see evidence of a passion for the glory of God in what you say? Can you say that you are at your best spiritually because certain men are in your life? If not, something is missing, and you've probably already felt it. If you see that passion in someone, you have a Jonathan, and it only gets better from here.

My Jonathan is named John Kiningham. On my pit crew, he is my fuel man. He can sense when I am running low or I'm on empty, and he is always there to fill me up. I am drawn to him because I see genuine love for Christ in him. I remember my first conversation with him, when he shared with me what he was learning from the book he was reading: Puritan Thomas Vincent's *The True Christian's Love to the Unseen Christ*. I noticed that whenever I heard him speak privately or publicly, he drew attention to Christ. When I listened to him pray, I wanted his closeness with the Savior. As I watched him interact with others, I felt that he was treating those people the way Christ would. For these reasons and more, I wanted to pull John closer to me so that I could be closer to Christ. Over the past 20 years, I have experienced his wise counsel, his timely warnings, and his genuine joy, and not once have I been disappointed. His example is the closest thing to this anonymous prayer:[3]

> Christ with me, Christ before me, Christ behind me, Christ within me, Christ beneath me, Christ above me, Christ on my right, Christ on my left, Christ when I lie down, Christ when I sit down, Christ when I arise, Christ in the heart of every man who thinks of me, Christ in the mouth of every one who speaks of me, Christ in every eye that sees me, Christ in every ear that hears me.

Draw near to the man who draws near to Christ. He will show you the way.

Quality #2: Affection

Affection? Sounds mushy, not manly. Incorrect. Some guys will roll their eyes at the idea of affection with other men. That's because they've misunderstood it or maybe have never experienced it. Intimacy between men sounds feminine and unnatural. Yet this description in the biblical text is repeated twice for emphasis: Jonathan "loved him as his own soul" (1 Samuel 18:1, 3).

To love someone as your own soul means to put his interests, needs, and wants before your own. It requires selflessness and imagination. You stop and think about what you would want, and then find your greatest joy in giving that away to your friend. Consider how much time and attention we give to ourselves. We take pretty good care of ourselves first. What if instead we did that for each other? Matthew 22:39 says, "You shall love your neighbor as yourself." And this requires an investment of time, energy, and resources. The more you put in, the more you get out.

God repeatedly draws attention to this love between David and Jonathan. Scripture shows us that men should have fond, warm, joyful affections for each other. Consider that day when Saul went crazy and plotted to murder David. When Jonathan set out to warn David, we get a glimpse of their affection. The text says, "David rose from beside the stone heap and fell on his face to the ground and bowed three times. And they *kissed* one another and wept with one another, David weeping the most" (1 Samuel 20:41).

Now don't get weirded out by this. They kissed, but not the way a man kisses a woman. Some have tried to use this as proof that David and Jonathan were gay. They weren't. Theirs was a different kind of love. David's attraction toward women is well documented, unfortunately. But the interaction between Jonathan and David does show that deep spiritual friendships display genuine affection.

You see it again at the end of Jonathan's life. David showed the depth of this affection after Jonathan's untimely death. He lamented, "I am distressed for you, my brother Jonathan; very pleasant have you been to me; your love to me was extraordinary, surpassing the love of women" (2 Samuel 1:26). It was a different kind of relationship, unlike those he had with his many wives. It got him through the hardest times, because "a friend loves at all times" (Proverbs 17:17).

Now let's be clear: The affection between men isn't designed to be the same as that in a man's relationship with his wife. A marriage relationship includes the erotic and romantic. Not so with dudes. We don't want to snuggle. We don't hold hands, share ice cream cones, dance, or try on clothes together. We work on projects together. We spot each other at the gym when the weights are heavy. We shoot guns with each other. We need time together, apart from the women in our lives. That's healthy. A bromance is not.

The affection will be different, but it will be there, and it will be real. You'll see strength, warmth, joy, gratitude, and support—all of which are backed up by the next quality.

Quality #3: Commitment

If friendship is anything, it is a commitment—an inward promise of loyalty, come what may. The text says that "Jonathan made a covenant with David" (1 Samuel 18:3). This is a serious element that is missing in our relationships today. Who make covenants? That feels like a bit much, doesn't it?

In the Bible, covenants refer to an agreement between two parties, like a contract. Each offers the other a promise, motivated by a penalty if either fails to uphold his end. Both parties called upon God to witness the vow, and once the covenant was confirmed, it became unalterable. You were to keep your end of the bargain whether you felt like it or not. Your relationship to God was the backstop for your pledge to the other person. If you faltered, you answered to God. Our friendships are fickle by comparison.

Have you ever had a guy say he was your friend, but he bailed on you when something or someone else came along? Who used you because he thought it would advance him forward, and you were a means to his end? Who abandoned you when he realized that your friendship would cost him more than he first anticipated? If so, you're not alone. Jesus had Judas, and Paul had Demas. Don't be that guy.

By contrast, when Jonathan wanted to show how loyal he was to David, he did something unthinkable. The text says, "Jonathan stripped himself of the robe that was on him and gave it to David, and his armor, and even his sword and his bow and his belt" (1 Samuel 18:4). In those days, it was common to give gifts in the making of a covenant, as a token of a promise. But realize what kind of robe, armor, and sword was being gifted to David. These were specially designed for the future king of Israel. This was a major expression of commitment!

Jonathan was the heir to the kingdom. These were royal accoutrements. The robe was sown to bear the dignity and beauty of majesty. The armor he gave to David was fashioned to protect the chest of the nation's leader. The sword, meant to lead the charge into battle, was most likely a magnificent weapon. In fact, it may have been somewhat unique because the Israelite army didn't even have swords; they used sharpened farm tools to fight (1 Samuel 13:19-20).

In giving these things to David, Jonathan voluntarily relinquished his right to the throne of Israel. This act was a declaration of lifelong loyalty to his new, future, God-appointed king. No self-preservation or self-promotion. Jonathan was dashing his own hopes of ruling over Israel. Who does that?

It seems likely Jonathan knew what had happened to his dad back in 1 Samuel 15–16. Because of Saul's sin, God had rejected him from being king and instead chose another to reign in his place. Jonathan watched his father turn into a jealous, cowardly, angry, demonic madman who refused to let go. Jonathan recognized God's hand on David, and perhaps concluded this was the man. In humble acceptance, he displayed the one virtue found in all true commitment—sacrifice.

Jonathan deferred so that a better man could take his place, all the while glad for the opportunity to step out of the way. He made sure David could flourish in God's plan. That takes amazing humility. This also tells us something about the true nature of commitment. A loyal friend remains devoted to you and is indifferent to the lure of prestige, position, and power.

A lesser friend would have been jealous and treacherous. Jonathan was handing off his dad's legacy, his own future. In effect, he got out of his race car and became the fuel man for the rest of his career. His new mission in life was to come over the wall with a full tank of gas and fill David up so that he could go the distance. Jonathan would never get behind the wheel again. No trophies, milk bottles, or victory laps. But he would savor the triumph just as much because of the role he would play.

What about you—are you this kind of friend? Beware that you don't become the guy who only takes and never gives. Commitment goes both ways. You should be striving to find as well as *be* a Jonathan. Take a minute and think about the level of loyalty you show to others. Do you give up your valuable time to bear a burden when you're exhausted? Do you put down your debit card to meet others' needs when your needs are just as pressing or greater? Do you use your platform to give someone else a start? Are you content to see your friends rise in status, popularity, and influence at the cost of your own? Friendship happens when you give yourself away.

Quality #4: Vulnerability

The commitment Jonathan and David made was tested from the start. As it became clear that God's hand was upon David, Saul became hostile toward the giant slayer. Unlike Jonathan, Saul was unwilling to lose his throne and would go to any length to avoid divine consequences. He was even willing to murder.

You can imagine how this put Jonathan in an awkward place. His dad wanted to kill his best friend. The evil king looked for any opportunity to exploit the relationship with his son to betray David. Jonathan would now have to walk the razor's edge. He would have to balance loyalty to his dad, Israel, God, and his covenant friend.

David's life was truly in Jonathan's hands. Thankfully, because of their friendship, David could place the full weight of his trust onto his friend. He knew that in spite of the pressure from Saul, Jonathan would do him good and not harm.

Jonathan was a safe place where David could be vulnerable. Proverbs 18:24 says, "There is a friend who sticks closer than a brother." Jonathan would prove to be that friend. You need someone who will protect you and your reputation, with whom you can be transparent. A Jonathan lets you be who you really are and loves you anyway. He covers you and protects you; he also stands there to support you. He guides you with his wisdom and accountability. You can trust your life in his hands even when you have no idea what might happen next.

It's like the game I sometimes play with my kids. I wrap a blindfold around one child's eyes and set him or her up in a room with all kinds of obstacles—toys, Legos, cups, whatever. My goal is to have that child listen to me as I verbally lead him or her through the slender paths without stumbling. As long as the child pays close attention to me and moves with caution, he or she makes it. But the hard part comes when I get the other kids to join in. Their job is to mislead the blindfolded one. They shout out different kinds of directions, of course, all designed to trip up their sibling. They try to drown out my voice.

But David, like my kids, learned to listen to a trusted voice. David knew that as long as he followed Jonathan's advice, he would survive. Consider this infamous event in 1 Samuel 19:

> Saul spoke to Jonathan his son and to all his servants, that they should kill David. But Jonathan, Saul's son, delighted much in David. And Jonathan told David, "Saul my father seeks to kill you. Therefore be on your guard in the

morning. Stay in a secret place and hide yourself. And I will go out and stand beside my father in the field where you are, and I will speak to my father about you. And if I learn anything I will tell you." And Jonathan spoke well of David to Saul his father and said to him, "Let not the king sin against his servant David, because he has not sinned against you, and because his deeds have brought good to you. For he took his life in his hand and he struck down the Philistine, and the LORD worked a great salvation for all Israel. You saw it, and rejoiced. Why then will you sin against innocent blood by killing David without cause?" And Saul listened to the voice of Jonathan. Saul swore, "As the LORD lives, he shall not be put to death." And Jonathan called David, and Jonathan reported to him all these things. And Jonathan brought David to Saul, and he was in his presence as before (verses 1-7).

Jonathan put his life on the line for David, and it worked. Saul turned away from his madness. Jonathan's intervention made the difference. No truce with treachery; true friends look out for each other.

But then there was a day when things didn't go so well. Later in the same chapter (19:8-18), Saul went nuts again and tried to skewer David with his spear as David was trying to soothe Saul with music. When David fled, the king set up a sting to kill him, using David's wife, Michal, who happened to be one of Saul's daughters. Thankfully, David's wife decided to help him escape, but that would be the end of their marriage. Saul would take Michal away and marry her to another man (25:44).

David became a man with no country, no home, and no wife. So where did he turn? Only one place was safe—his best friend. And when he turned to Jonathan, notice how David was vulnerable in yet another way:

David fled from Naioth in Ramah and came and said before Jonathan, "What have I done? What is my guilt? And what is my sin before your father, that he seeks my life?" And he said to him, "Far from it! You shall not die. Behold, my father does nothing either great or small without disclosing it to me. And why should my father hide this from me? It is not so." But David vowed again, saying, "Your father knows well that I have found favor in your eyes, and he thinks, 'Do not let Jonathan know this, lest he be grieved.' But truly, as the LORD lives and as your soul lives, there is but a step between me and death." Then Jonathan said to David, "Whatever you say, I will do for you" (1 Samuel 20:1-4).

Did you catch that? David was in danger of being assassinated, but his primary concern wasn't his own protection. Rather, he opened his soul to Jonathan and made himself accountable in matters of sin. To David, personal holiness was more important than his life. He was completely candid and broken before a friend whom he knew would love him enough to tell him the truth.

In this frenzy, David was more eager to examine his spiritual condition than he was to get relief from his circumstances. "What have I done? What is my guilt? And what is my sin…?" Some guys don't think about these things. They don't want to take responsibility for their actions. By contrast, godly men care about the condition of their own hearts and invite other godly men into their struggles. They seek men who will shoot straight with them.

Three Kinds of Friends

You have three kinds of friends in your life. Those who have (1) a *view* of your life, (2) a *voice* in your life, and (3) a *vote* in your life. Those who have a *view* tend to be acquaintances—they can see what's happening and they may have an opinion, but it may or may not be helpful. They sit in the cheap seats like the outfield crowd at a baseball game.

Those with a *voice* are people you respect and who have access to you. They are close enough to speak into the situations you face. Usually what they say is helpful, but you still weigh their advice and may or may not follow it. They're watching you from behind home plate and yelling out their support.

Those with a *vote* are like Jonathan. You listen to them and do what they say. They are in your dugout, sending hand signals that help you know what to do. They stand at third base, telling you whether to run or slide into home base. Their goal is to keep you from getting tagged out. Even if their counsel goes against your emotions, you've learned to trust their judgment. You know they love you and would never steer you wrong.

Do you have a guy like this in your life? Someone with whom you can be real, who can see you at your worst? A trustworthy brother is willing to give you feedback about your soul. A proven friend isn't going to exploit your vulnerabilities and use them against you.

If you've been burned in the past, having this kind of trust is hard to do. I've learned to be suspicious of people who let me be real with them but don't share their struggles in return. Sometimes it's because they haven't learned how necessary that is to spiritual growth. Other times it's because they relish gaining an advantage over you, a twisted form of power. My experience with men who won't be vulnerable is they eventually abandon or betray you. Don't entrust yourself to that kind of person. Don't waste your time. Find a Jonathan instead.

At every opportunity, Jonathan "strengthened [David's] hand in God" (1 Samuel 23:16). But as he covered David's vulnerabilities, he became vulnerable too. Throughout the rest of his life, Jonathan put himself on the line for David, and eventually it would cost him his life. Protecting David meant insults, isolation, and dodging spears from his psycho dad. But it was worth it.

The story tragically ends in 1 Samuel 31, with Jonathan fighting alongside his doomed father. David's best friend met his demise in battle. When the news reached David's ears, it became one of the most painful losses in his life.

Want to hear something sad? As long as Saul was alive, David and Jonathan rarely saw each other. These best friends didn't get much time to enjoy their friendship. Not until they reunited in heaven were they able to do that. But that doesn't mean their friendship had any less impact on their lives.

Just Enough Fuel to Finish

As his fuel man, Jonathan made sure David never ran out of gas, though I'm sure there were times when David got nervous because the "low fuel" light had been on for a while. Yet right on time, every time, Jonathan was exactly what David needed. God made sure that the last time Jonathan came over the wall for David, the final fill-up would be enough to send David across the finish line.

When Jonathan died, David lamented and rightly so. But he took the memory of his friend and the lessons they had learned together into his future. David knew he would see Jonathan again. They would have a friendship in heaven better than they ever had on earth. While on earth, they could let one another go because they both knew the one who had brought them together. That friendship was still intact and stronger than ever because of each other. When you read the Psalms and see how close David was to God, a major part of that is because Jonathan had been in his life. He helped

David draw near to God in the midst of difficult days, and God took over where Jonathan left off.

You might already have a Jonathan in your life, and if so, keep going. Never take him for granted. Press in. Even if he lives far away and you don't get much time together, find ways to strengthen each other in God.

If you don't have a Jonathan, stop now and ask God for this incredible gift and start looking around you for the answer. He is not hard to spot. He is the guy who is passionate about God and is willing to follow Him even when no one else will. So what if he has different tastes in lifestyle, music, sports, cars, or food. *Fuhgeddaboudit.* Find a Jonathan.

Important Takeaways to Remember

- We are vulnerable when we are alone.
- A biblical friend is someone who joins you on a journey as both companion and guide, whom you can trust, respect, and enjoy along the way.
- All biblical friendships are rooted in the mutual desire to see God glorified above all else.
- God's glory refers to His heaviness and weightiness. Our best friends should be those who show us how much God matters.
- Strong men can and should have fond, warm, joyful affections for each other, different from a man's affection for a woman. Don't be afraid to express godly emotions with other men.
- A loyal friend remains devoted to you and is indifferent to the lure of prestige, position, and power.
- There are three kinds of friends in your life: those with a view, a voice, and a vote. Those with a view have an opinion, but it may or may not be helpful. Those with a voice are close enough to speak into the situations you face and may or may not have good advice. Those with a vote are like Jonathan. Even if their counsel goes against your emotions, you can trust their judgment to steer you the right direction.

Finding Your Jonathan

Most guys have someone they can point to as a best friend, but that doesn't mean that friend is a Jonathan. Each of us typically has someone who is closer to us than others, but the key is whether that connection is nurturing on a spiritual level. A Jonathan is a man who leaves you feeling refreshed, emboldened, and invigorated every time you are together. You're happier and holier because of him. As you survey your sphere of influence, consider the following questions to help you discover and utilize your Jonathan.

1. Jonathan found David because he recognized David's zeal for the glory of God. Would you say this is your passion, strong enough for all to see? If so, your Jonathan will find you. Describe your commitment to God in the following areas. Circle the ones that need the most attention, and write some simple steps you can take to improve in those areas:

- The boundaries you have with the opposite sex.

- The guard you place on the use of your time.

- The ambitions you have for your career.

- The control you exercise over your temper.

- The attitude you have toward those who irritate or injure you.

2. One major roadblock to a David/Jonathan relationship is the view that affection is womanish. Are you adverse to showing

your emotions to others perhaps because it makes you feel weak? If so, you probably aren't expressing yourself truly and helpfully to the Lord either. Might that be the case? Read a few of the Psalms and see the way David expressed intense emotions, both high and low. Set a time this week to get alone and genuinely pour out your heart before the Lord (Psalm 62:8) and start this new pattern of showing affection to Him. You'll know you have a Jonathan when you can process with him like this.

3. Jonathan's pledge of love and loyalty to David was not only serious in its commitment, but it also cost Jonathan everything: his family, his safety, his throne, and ultimately, his life. As you think about the guys in your life, ask yourself: Are they flighty or faithful? In the space below, write down— in your own words—the characteristics of a faithful friend. From today onward, start sticking with the men who do what they say. You don't have time for those who are fickle.

4. How truthful are you? Of course, this refers to whether you intentionally deceive or mislead others, but a Jonathan/David

relationship depends on far more. It requires you to evaluate how open and transparent you are with other men about the areas in which you struggle. Is there an area of your life in which you are falling down and hiding the problem from others? Don't forfeit the blessings of walking in the light of accountability (John 3:20-21). Pick up the phone and call your Jonathan—he is your lifeline (Joshua 7:19).

CHAPTER 4

You Need a Courageous Brother to Confront You

Have you ever had one of those days when you knew you were beginning to see your sin in a new way? You know, when you find yourself thinking, *Am I really this wretched? Did I really just do that? Did those words actually come out of my mouth?* I had such a day, and I remember it vividly.

I had a bad argument with my wife and I needed to get out of the house. I don't think I had ever been that angry before in our marriage. I had said some of the most hurtful things I've ever uttered. I was so hardened in my heart that I was finding it hard to repent. I needed help. I drove to a monastery where I was sure no one would know me, and I walked the grounds until dusk. I needed to clear my mind, pull out of the emotion, and be alone with God. After about an hour and a half, having stoked my hope in the cross, I walked back to my car.

I looked at my cell phone still in the cupholder. It indicated that

I had missed one call and one voicemail. I clicked on my cell to listen to the message: "Hey Justin, it's Dave. My wife and I spent some time tonight talking with Jana. Sounds like you guys have had a rough night. Can you give me a call?"

My wife told on me? I wasn't mad. I knew that I had offended my bride and that she loved me in spite of my hardness of heart. She knew, based on my last state of mind, it was better to have someone else reach out to me than her—another man. She was right. I'm glad she did.

Then I listened to the voicemail: "Hey brother...I've been praying for you...I love you...I know what Spirit dwells in you...I've been there..." Dave Fry is one of those guys I can call no matter what time of day or night it is. I can tell him anything, good or bad. And my wife still calls him on occasion as well. His wife calls me too. Dave and I have the kind of friendship where we refuse to let each other go down in a fireball.

We need Daves in our lives who will press in on us, who love us enough to ask the hard questions. We are in trouble without brothers who care more about our holiness than about offending us. We need a guy who is willing to be harder on our sin than we are. That's what God says in Proverbs 12:1: "Whoever loves discipline loves knowledge, but he who hates reproof is stupid." Later in Proverbs 29:1 we read, "A man who hardens his neck after much reproof will suddenly be broken beyond remedy" (NASB).

In the Bible, the concept of rebuke means confronting sin so that we feel the weight of its seriousness before God. It means to make a case against someone, to show that he is in the wrong, and to come under God's authority. The challenge is to let men into our lives whom we know will help us recognize the need to change. Whenever that's needed, they're ready.

Don't get me wrong—getting rebuked is not fun. Even the word *rebuke* sounds like *puke,* like you just got something gross all over you. While rebuke can get messy, God says it is good for us. Consider what the following verses teach about how we should treat sin in us and in others:

> Matthew 18:15: "If your brother sins against you, go and tell him his fault, between you and him alone. If he listens to you, you have gained your brother."

> Ephesians 5:11: "Take no part in the unfruitful works of darkness, but instead expose them."

These verses reveal how we are made to depend on others who care for us on a spiritual level. We need friends who are willing to tell us the truth about our sin whether we like it or not. If we are going to grow, then we cannot resist their willingness to be forthright and let us feel the weight of conviction that God wants to place on our hearts.

The Man We Need When We Set Ourselves on Fire

King David had the ultimate example of this in his life—he had Nathan. This guy friend played a vital role in helping David, a man after God's own heart, at a time when that wasn't so important to him. There was a day when David lost control of the wheel and crashed and burned. At this time, he needed one of his most important guy friends: his fire extinguisher. The story appears in 2 Samuel 12.

Sadly, by this point in his life, David was already a compromised man. The little sins he had been committing had been adding up. He was a spiritual casualty waiting to happen. It all started when he decided to stay home while his army went into battle. Laziness lulled him into having an idle mind. The 50-year-old king woke up in the *evening* from a nap, wandered onto his rooftop, and saw a woman bathing. Why she was there is a story for another time.

Aroused with a sinful curiosity, David inquired about her. Bad plan. He should've run the other way. Once he learned her name, Bathsheba, he realized that she was married. Her husband was Uriah, one of David's 30 mighty men who had sworn to protect him during the years of Saul's madness (1 Chronicles 11:41). Her dad was one of these mighty men as well (2 Samuel 23:34). These guys were personal bodyguards, a kind of elite secret service, a special-ops task force. They would have taken a spear to the chest for David and counted it as their highest honor.

One more thing: Bathsheba's husband, Uriah, was a Hittite. That means he was once a godless man. He came from the people group that had endured the longest-standing feud with Israel (Genesis 15:20). Somewhere along the line, Uriah became a follower of the one true God, having denied his upbringing, his people, and his religion. In short, his faith had cost him everything.

But that didn't matter to David. He had a wretched passion burning in his heart that he would not extinguish. A bigger giant than Goliath was calling his name, a giant in his heart named lust. Foolishly, acting on his impulses, he sent for Bathsheba, slept with her, and got her pregnant. Not his finest moment.

Rather than confess and forsake his sin of adultery, David concocted what he thought was the perfect deception. To cover up his sin, David summoned Uriah home from the battle. He pretended he wanted to learn how the battle was going and to thank Uriah for fighting. To honor Uriah, he sent him home to rest for a little while, eat, and be with his wife. And you know what hard-working, battle-weary men want to do with their wives after a couple of months away, right? It was the perfect cover-up. *Everyone would think the baby was Uriah's.*

The only problem was Uriah was too loyal. He refused to go home. Instead, he slept outside the palace with the servants. What happened next was vile. David, in effect, said, "You want to be a devoted solider? You want to be back in the battle instead of being an accomplice to my little tryst? You want to be out in the fray? Request granted."

David penned Uriah's death sentence on a scroll, rolled it up, dribbled some official wax on the scroll so it would stay shut, pressed the wax with his official signet, and gave the letter to Uriah to take back to the general. In this secret order, David commanded his general to put Uriah in the front of the battle to fight all by himself. Meanwhile the rest of the army was to move back, leaving Uriah on the battlefield to die alone, which he did. Evil. Pure evil. Just as David planned.

David's orders were executed perfectly. Worse still, to compensate for the loss, David played the role of compassionate hero. He flew the flag at half mast, so to speak, and took the widow of his trusted friend into his house. He made her his wife. What's one more? He already had 22. *Oh, how sweet. And look, they have a honeymoon baby! He's a preemie, but what a benevolent king. She will never have to worry about a thing for the rest of her life.* David came out smelling like a rose, but the stench of his high-handed rebellion reached all the way to heaven, and it reeked.

At least nine months, maybe a year went by, and the dirty little secret was safe. That is, until God sent Nathan the prophet to confront him. It's here that Nathan shows us what to do in those times when we have to make the hard choice to do the hard thing to keep one another from having a hard heart. Nathan models the necessary ingredients to a successful confrontation. This is how it's supposed to look:

Ingredient #1: A Nathan Is Already Proven Trustworthy as a Friend

The text opens with these simple words in 2 Samuel 12:1: "The LORD sent Nathan to David." Now, Nathan wasn't just anybody. He was David's trusted, faithful confidant and counselor. He was also a prophet of God, which means that he was the man responsible to tell David whatever God said.

Nathan had been on hand at the highest point of David's life, when God made His covenant with David (2 Samuel 7). That day, God promised that in the future, Jesus Himself would reign on David's throne over all the earth. Nathan had been with David for a while, and he had already proven to be a faithful friend. It makes sense, then, that when David needed to hear about his sin, Nathan was the logical choice for a spokesman. God sent the man who had a time-tested relationship with David.

On this day, David would have to learn what Proverbs 27:5-6 says: "Better is open rebuke than hidden love. Faithful are the wounds of a friend; profuse are the kisses of an enemy." This means it is better for someone to openly blast you for your sin than to say nothing and gloss over what you've done. Someone who smothers you with kisses, while withholding what you need to hear, is not your friend. He's your enemy. A friend does what is in your best interest whether you like it or not, whether you ask for it or not.

In one sense, this friend is like a surgeon. Have you ever had surgery? If so, do you realize that you actually paid someone a large sum of money to cut you? That person slashed you and made you bleed. He may have caused you a significant amount of pain. You may have had to take several days or even weeks to recover. You paid him to hurt you. You even thanked him afterward for what he had done. Why? Because you knew he hurt you in order to *heal* you.

The same is true in the spiritual realm. The incision of rebuke ultimately promotes healing in your soul. The scalpel of reproof, rightly applied to the cancer of sin, is just what the Great Physician ordered. Nathan was this kind of friend, proven in his love and loyalty long before he had to "get in David's kitchen."

Your Nathan is someone who knows you because you let him in. You don't hold him at arm's length or give superficial answers to probing questions. You look him in the eyes and tell him the truth—all of it. You also ask him to look over your shoulder into your blind spots so you don't crash. He's not there to police you, but he is close enough to see what you are really like when your guard is down. He leans in and you don't push back against him. Your Nathan is so much more than someone who confronts you, but he is not less.

Ingredient #2: A Nathan Is More Loyal to God Than He Is to You

This is so subtle it's easy to miss: "The LORD sent Nathan to David. He came to him and said…" (2 Samuel 12:1). This may have been the hardest thing God had asked this prophet to do. Truthfully, confronting David would have been terrifying. After all, David was the king. He was the head of the nation, the source of power, rule, and authority. He led the most blessed and prosperous land in the world. But he had also proven treacherous to anyone who would threaten to expose the cover-up. He had one of his best friends snuffed out.

Nathan had to have been nervous. He knew David could turn

against him and send him to a similar fate as Uriah. He knew that confronting David would result in a public scandal, and that the enemies of the Lord would blaspheme God because of David's behavior. The model of what it meant to be a man after God's heart had been shattered. The prophet could have been tempted to stay silent. He could have tried to excuse David to avoid the confrontation. But he could not. Nathan was more loyal to the King of kings than to the king of Israel.

Now, God doesn't reveal other people's sins to us with prophetic utterances, but He does reveal them. And He does command us to reprove those who are in sin (Galatians 6:1-2; 1 Thessalonians 5:14; Titus 1:13). We *have* to go. There will be times in our lives when we are forced to decide whether we will fear God or man (Proverbs 29:25; Galatians 1:10). Confrontation is hard, but necessary. It doesn't matter the position, rank, or influence of the person we are about to face. We must have a loyalty to God over our loyalty to our friends. That's where we will find courage.

Be careful, though. Don't be a spiritual gestapo. We're not talking about doing spur-of-the-moment bed checks on the people in your life. We aren't called to hunt them down and find out what skeletal remains are in their closets. We're talking about helping those who are endangering themselves with unrepentant sins. We're talking about intervening for good, with grace and truth, like a doctor does.

David had a spiritual staph infection that started with one small tear in the skin of his character. Untreated, this infection had spread all the way to his heart. This is triage. No time to wait. Nathan was a man under divine mandate. God said, "Go," and it wasn't optional. It's not optional for us either. God is not interested in whether we feel like giving rebuke or receiving it. You need to remember that when Nathan calls your phone. Once Nathan has resolved to be obedient to God, it's only a matter of what to say and how. Nathan's example helps us there too.

Ingredient #3: A Nathan Is Careful and Clear in His Communication

What happens next is both shrewd and genius. Nathan doesn't just burst into the throne room with guns blazing. He contains his emotions and doesn't do anything careless. He tells David a little story.

The parable is about sheep. If you recall, David used to care for sheep and defend them against lions and bears. He helped birth little ewes, carried them from pasture to pasture, fed them and nursed them. He had been a full-fledged shepherd and not a mere hireling, which is why Nathan's little spiel would tug on his heart. Selfishly, the rich man in the story had stolen someone else's only sheep and killed it to indulge a traveling stranger, when he had plenty of his own sheep to draw from. Nathan was presenting a parallel to what David had done, but David didn't know it yet.

At first you might think Nathan was being cryptic rather than clear. But if you watch closely, you'll see he was waiting for just the right moment for the takedown. He was like a skilled boxer waiting for the right angle to present itself so he could land the uppercut that would result in a knockout. It wouldn't likely happen in the first round. It didn't have to.

Nathan made David think about the situation without bias toward himself. Realize that David didn't know this was a made-up story. It probably sounded like Nathan was asking him for an official ruling for a civil dispute. Maybe the king thought he was being asked for input on what should happen to a citizen in his kingdom who had done this. That seems to be how David took it, according to 2 Samuel 12:5-6:

> David's anger was greatly kindled against the man, and he said to Nathan, "As the LORD lives, the man who has done this deserves to die, and he shall restore the lamb fourfold, because he did this thing, and because he had no pity."

That's great, David! *He should die. Then he should repay four times the amount.* David was furious. Isn't that us sometimes? We can see the lesser sins in others as more hideous than the greater sins in ourselves!

But here is ultimate hypocrisy, and it's why Nathan presented the situation to David in the form of a story. David had just sentenced himself. What he had just condemned was completely true of *him*. And once Nathan established a baseline for accountability, he lowered the boom. He spoke with absolute clarity: "You are the man!" (verse 7). No ambiguity there.

Now David could see that the poor man in the story was Uriah. Bathsheba was the little lamb that David, the rich man, had stolen. The famished guest was the lust in David's heart, and he had fed it until he was full.

Pause here long enough to realize that we need Nathans because our hearts are deceitful (Jeremiah 17:9). Our consciences do not always work right (1 Corinthians 4:4). We need men like Nathan who are willing to confront us so that we see ourselves in light of God's holiness.

We don't need men who drop hints and subtle nuances, who never get to the heart of the matter because they are afraid to be forthright with us. We need men who are willing to work hard to be as clear as possible when we need to be challenged toward holy living. Godliness is a team effort.

We don't need men who drop hints and subtle nuances, who never get to the heart of the matter because they are afraid to be forthright with us. **We need men who are willing to work hard to be as clear as possible when we need to be challenged toward holy living.** Godliness is a team effort.

Ingredient #4: A Nathan Doesn't Sugarcoat What God Says

Nathan was gutsy and obedient, which translates into boldness. Speaking for the Lord, he said:

> I anointed you king over Israel, and I delivered you out of the hand of Saul. And I gave you your master's house and your master's wives into your arms and gave you the house of Israel and of Judah. And if this were too little, I would add to you as much more. Why have you despised the word of the LORD, to do what is evil in his sight? You have struck down Uriah the Hittite with the sword and have taken his wife to be your wife and have killed him with the sword of the Ammonites (2 Samuel 12:7-9).

Nathan threw that verbal uppercut, and it connected. He didn't dance around the ring and shadowbox. He found the right moment and, in a flash, landed the punch square on David's jaw, putting him on the mat. No need to count to ten; David wasn't getting up.

Nathan's rebuke could be summarized as follows: "Your gross ingratitude led you to squander divine privileges, and you did this because you hated the word of God, and most of all, you hated God Himself!" Nathan didn't give a fair name to foul sins. He reproached David for doing "what is evil" in God's sight (verse 9). David found himself on the other side of the truth he once proclaimed:

> O LORD my God, if I have done this, if there is wrong in my hands, if I have repaid my friend with evil or plundered my enemy without cause, let the enemy pursue my soul and overtake it, and let him trample my life to the ground and lay my glory in the dust (Psalm 7:3-5).

There David lay, not at the hands of an enemy, but of a faithful friend. That friend had said some hard things. David had to hear what he was unwilling to think in the moment of temptation and pleasure: God was angry. The calluses that had built up on his heart were getting ripped off, and David was bleeding and oozing, but finally penitent. One day, he would be glad for this.

Ingredient #5: A Nathan Is Sober About the Reality of Sin's Consequences

For the first time in a long while, David was starting to ache and throb inside, and it was a good thing. He was beginning to absorb months' worth of guilt. His mind was overrun with sorrow.

God's words were still ringing in his boxed ears: "You despised Me." The malignancy Nathan had cut out was huge, and David was starting to get better, but he was still stinging. No spiritual morphine. And that wasn't all. David had barely begun to feel the effects of his sin. The pain was going to get much worse, and it would last the rest of his life. And who was there again to deliver that news? Nathan.

> Now therefore the sword shall never depart from your house, because you have despised me and have taken the wife of Uriah the Hittite to be your wife. Thus says the LORD, "Behold, I will raise up evil against you out of your own house. And I will take your wives before your eyes and give them to your neighbor, and he shall lie with your wives in the sight of this sun. For you did it secretly, but I will do this thing before all Israel and before the sun...Nevertheless, because by this deed you have utterly scorned the LORD, the child who is born to you shall die" (2 Samuel 12:10-12, 14).

You are going to spend the rest of your life suffering the consequences of your sin. You will learn that God is not mocked—whatever a man sows, that he will reap (Galatians 6:7). Ouch!

Sound severe? Sin has consequences. The sobering truth for us as men is this: Even though God may forgive you, the aftereffects of sin can remain. God might take that hard, stony sin out of your heart and throw it to the bottom of the sea, but the ripples on the surface will continue to spread outward until they reach the shore. Someone had to tell David. Who better than Nathan?

As personal as David's sin was to God, it would now be that personal to David. *David's* wives would be plundered, *David's* child would die, and *David's* house would be torn apart. These consequences were personal, painful, and proportionate. But they were also purposeful. God was sending a message to David's heart that can only come this way.

The same is true with us—the pain has to outweigh the pleasure to discourage us from going back to the sin again. This is good and necessary for God to do for us. Discipline is extremely effective, especially if it hits home in a personal way. Sin leaves a scar that reminds us of its devastation, which, in turn, helps us to continue in repentance.

The Nathans in your life are there to warn you about the awfulness of sin. They aren't there to cushion the blow that God intends to use so you turn away from the sin. They know that to lessen the anguish of sin is to short-circuit your repentance. They are unwilling to let that happen. Yet they are not all severity. They know how to give hope too. That's where Nathan went next.

Ingredient #6: A Nathan Gives the Hope and Comfort of Grace

Nathan's rebuke didn't stand alone. Once he saw David humble himself, Nathan rushed in with hope. The king had just been told that he was going to lose much that he held dear. It probably would have been easier if he had been stoned to death, which was the Bible's penalty for adulterers and murderers. Facing the future wasn't going to be easy. David's wrongdoing was going to be made public. But God would impart His grace to David, and Nathan would convey that assurance. "David said to Nathan, 'I have sinned against the Lord.' And Nathan said to David, 'The Lord also has put away your sin; you shall not die'" (2 Samuel 12:13). David saw another side of Nathan—his hopeful side.

As firm and severe as Nathan had been, he was just as quick to pronounce the hope that is found in God's grace. Men like this understand that repentance results in *immediate* forgiveness from God. They also know that if we don't have hope, our repentance won't last long. They know how to point us to verses like Proverbs 28:13: "Whoever conceals his transgressions will not prosper, but he who confesses and forsakes them will obtain mercy." And 1 John 1:9: "If we confess our sins, he is faithful and just to forgive us our sins and to cleanse us from all unrighteousness."

It's important that we have these promises at the moment of our deepest regret, like lifeboats after we've sunk our own ships. We want to be reminded that God does not love us because of the good we do or how well we clean up. Rather, He loves us because He has chosen to love us (see Deuteronomy 7:7) and has forgiven us in Christ. We need to remember that He is for us and the cross has already resolved our sin problem (Romans 8:1). A Nathan will give you hope right when you need it, and not a moment too soon or too late. Then he can leave you with God to do the rest.

That's why Nathan did what he did next: "Then Nathan went to his house" (verse 15). At first this might sound kind of cold, but David needed to be alone with the Lord. The psalmist hadn't written in a while. He needed to pen Psalm 51, then Psalm 32. The prophet was stepping back so God could step in. But this is not the last we see of Nathan.

Ingredient #7: A Nathan Remains Faithful in His Commitment to You

Just as Nathan had been with David before this incident, so he would continue with him afterward. Nathan was committed to David to the end. Our fear is that when people know us truly, the real us, they will pull away. It's why we sometimes don't go deep and share when we should. As men, we like the view people have of us from a distance. We look better from afar. But given what God was about to do in David's life, Nathan was going to need a faithful friend to stand with him. Amazingly, Nathan was that man again.

In the same chapter in which Nathan devastated his king, he showed up again, at the birth of Solomon. If you recall, this child was the product of a union that never should have been. He was David and Bathsheba's little boy. In spite of this, Nathan was there. He assured this couple that the Lord loved this little guy and would make something of him. Solomon would be king one day, and through his line, Messiah would come to reign forever.

Later, in 1 Kings 1, at the end of David's life, as he drew his final breaths, the kingdom swirled with controversy. Political tension was mounting and insurrections were forming. The king was helpless and vulnerable, and it was Nathan who helped him lead the nation back into peace. When it mattered most, one man stood in the gap and made the difference for David: Nathan. The same man who had sent David to the mat spitting teeth.

Nathan was true to David, loyal to the end, in bad times and good. He showed no hint of resentment or bitterness. Nathan stayed by David's side as a friend, faithful to the last.

Close Enough to Put Your Fire Out

Who are the men God has raised up to speak into your life? Do they know what's going on with you under the hood? Do you pull them in? Are they close enough to put your fires out? You are flammable.

Race cars can catch on fire easily, and irreparable damage can occur quickly. Once flames engulf the car, the driver has only a few seconds to get out with his life. Often a fire is a total loss. Do a Google search for "NASCAR fires" or "NASCAR explosions." Watch the top hits to see what I mean. You'll feel like you can't watch, but you can't look away. Some guys don't realize they are on fire until their car explodes, sending debris into the crew, injuring the very people who are trying to help the drivers. Don't be that guy. Make sure you find a Nathan. He's holding the fire extinguisher. He's made for this.

Important Takeaways to Remember

- There are some days when you will truly be the worst sinner you know. A Nathan is the kind of person you can turn to in those times.

- Rebuke means confronting sin so that we feel the weight of its seriousness before God and come under His authority. The challenge is to let men into our lives whom we know will help us recognize the need to change.

- It is better for someone to openly blast you for your sin than to say nothing. Someone who smothers you with kisses while withholding what you need to hear is not your friend. He's your enemy.

- Your Nathan is so much more than someone who confronts you, but he is not less.

- We have to be careful in our relationships with others that we don't become a spiritual gestapo. We're helping someone who is endangering himself with unrepentant sin.

- Even though God may forgive you, the consequences of sin can remain. Those consequences will be personal, painful, and proportionate. But they will also be purposeful.

Finding Your Nathan

Do a mental scan of the guys you've called or hung out with the most over the last three months. Is there a Nathan in the group? You'll be able to spot him because he's not a man-pleaser, but forthright, confidential, and practical. You'll hear him make personal applications of God's truth to his own life. He's also able to tell you what needs to be said because he cares about God's glory and your holiness. The following questions will help you find and utilize your fire extinguisher.

1. Do you have someone you think you could call at 3:00 a.m. if needed—someone who, even if you woke him up, would speak truth and pray for you so that you don't fall into temptation? Write his name below, shoot him a text, tell him what you're learning in this chapter, and ask if he would be available under those circumstances.

2. The best accountability is self-initiated, when you are willing to divulge how often and where you are struggling. Instead of waiting for someone to track you down, be willing to uncover anything you are hiding from the other guys in your life or trying to manage on your own. What do you need to be honest about and get into the open? (See John 3:19-21).

3. David was taken out by lust, but as we know, he had already been a compromised man for some time. His big sins came on the heels of many little sins that had accumulated over time. As you think about your life, write down five areas in which you are tempted to make little compromises. Then invite your Nathan to help you stop the progression of sin (read Hebrews 3:13) in these areas.

4. Is there any part of you that doesn't feel like you need a Nathan, that makes you think you can handle a specific struggle on your own? Is it possible that you've found excuses to justify holding other men at arm's length while pretending everything is okay? Debunk each the following sin-rationalizing statements below and then circle the top two you hear yourself saying:

- "It's not that bad." *Response:*

- "It won't happen to me." *Response:*

- "No one will know." *Response:*

- "I am not hurting anyone." *Response:*

- "I can stop anytime I want." *Response:*

- "It's too strong; I can't resist it." *Response:*

- "God wants me to be happy, and I deserve it." *Response:*

5. Now look at the two excuses you've circled and determine, in greater depth, why they are not valid:

CHAPTER 5

You Need a Faithful Disciple to Follow You

At first it might seem like another chapter on mentoring is redundant. Having already described Paul's role as a mentor to Timothy back in chapter 1, it would be easy for me to say, "Just read that chapter again, and this time, imagine yourself as the mentor, and not the one being mentored."

But it's not as simple as that. When you look for a Paul to serve as a role model for you, you're looking for an example you can imitate. By contrast, when you look for a Timothy whom you can train up, that's an entirely different angle from which to view the friendship. It's like trying to describe a table—the vantage point from the top is different than the view from underneath. Same table, different angle.

I've also placed this chapter here intentionally for this reason: If you take seriously everything that is written in chapters 1-4, you are becoming the kind of man who can and should start giving himself to mentoring, especially because as a growing Christian, you have something to offer.

In the pit crew, your Timothy is your jack-man. You can't win without him. He comes underneath you to lift you up, even though others might be working on different parts of your car. If you find the right guy, he's not a drain on you. He does his job and speeds you on your way. In the process he learns what he needs to know until the day he takes the wheel. It's a win for both of you.

Taking the Guesswork out of Mentoring

When it comes to choosing the person you would mentor, you need to know what to look for. There are certain qualities that ensure a good match for you. You also need to know what to do with the disciple once you find him so you can make the best use of your time together. There are certain benefits you will receive from having a Timothy in your life—this friendship will contribute to your ongoing development as a man of God. With those things in mind, I've listed some questions you can ask in your search for a Timothy. As you go through the questions, remember this: Jesus said the greatest way to make an impact on the world is to disciple someone. Discipleship is the start and finish of Jesus's Great Commission.

> Go therefore and *make disciples of all nations*, baptizing them in the name of the Father and of the Son and of the Holy Spirit, teaching them to observe all that I have commanded you. And behold, I am with you always, to the end of the age (Matthew 28:19-20, emphasis added).

Disciple-making is our mission, and it's simple. If a man doesn't know God, help him come to a saving relationship through Jesus Christ. If he surrenders his life to Christ, stand with him as he openly declares Jesus as Lord, then teach him all that Jesus has commanded. If you encounter someone who is already a believer but is spiritually younger, you are in a place to help him learn how to be a better follower of Christ. This is how the legacy of Christianity is passed from one generation to the next.

Everywhere he's been in the last decade, apologist Josh McDowell has sounded the alarm, "Christianity is always one generation away from extinction." He's absolutely right. Now, we know Jesus promised, "I will build my church, and the gates of hell shall not prevail against it" (Matthew 16:18), so Christianity is never going to become extinct. However, McDowell's point is well taken and creates a sense of urgency for us—true Christian hope cannot be passed on from one generation to the next without discipleship. History provides many examples of entire cultures, nations, and generations of people who did not have the Christian hope made available to them because the previous generation failed to pass it on. Just ask the people of Nineveh, who repented at the preaching of Jonah, whose children perished only one generation later (see the Old Testament book of Nahum). It comes down to this: Pass it on, or get passed over. (Here's where you say, "Not on my watch.")

All we have to do is nothing, and the spiritual heritage that has been entrusted to us will expire with us. But the reason Jesus chose disciples in the first place was to ensure His work would continue through the ages. That's why Paul told Timothy in 2 Timothy 2:2, "What you have heard from me in the presence of many witnesses entrust to faithful men, who will be able to teach others also." Notice the four generations that receive and pass on the legacy of faith: Paul to Timothy, Timothy to faithful/able men, and faithful/able men to those they teach. This is the clearest statement in Scripture on our responsibility to teach others and bring them to spiritual maturity. It also answers the most important questions we're asking about discipleship.

Question 1: What should you look for in someone you would disciple?

This question needs a specific answer because we are called to "make disciples of all nations." This is everyone, everywhere. But as you think of a starting line, Paul (our example) says look for "faithful men who will be able to teach others also." That's who you disciple—those who are faithful and able. This does not mean that you should hold off on discipling someone until he has grown for a while. *Faithful* and *able* are qualities immediately discernible, even in brand new believers. Rick Holland, one of my mentors, frequently said, "It's never about how long you've been in the boat; it's about how hard you row." I know many young believers who are doing laps around some who have been in the boat quite a bit longer.

Paul's use of the word "faithful" speaks of consistency. This is the ability to follow through. A faithful disciple makes himself available, takes on responsibilities, and carries them out. He doesn't slack off or make excuses. He knows the costs of negligence and complacency and doesn't quit. You know he is worth the time you put into him because he is reliable. More men like this, please! (see Psalms 12:1; 101:6).

"Able" refers to competency. This person can actually do what you ask of him. He is motivated to learn what he needs to know and rises to the occasion. He can handle the responsibilities he takes on and stays at them with focus, determination, and zeal. He is eager and has the capacity to put things into action.

Men without consistency and competency are like cars with bad gas mileage—you can never get very far with them. Too often you have to pull off the road just when you thought you were getting somewhere. Some new distraction, some new issue, some new reason why they aren't changing. They not only fail to reach their spiritual destination, they slow you down and keep you from investing in men who want to grow.

This was my experience with one man I was discipling—let's call him Herman. Herman was having life problems, interpersonal problems, marriage problems, kid problems, work problems, and health problems. He would sit with me for hours, sharing his woes and looking for relief. I met with Herman consistently, taught him the Bible, showed him the heart issues behind his problems, gave him practical examples of things he could do, and supported him with others in his life who could remind and encourage him to do the right thing.

I did everything I could to help motivate Herman, but nothing seemed to work. Each week, Herman came back and was worse off than before. But one day, as he started into his sad story of the-world-against-me-as-a-reason-why-I-should-not-be-expected-to-change, I stopped him and pointed out that for all the time invested in our meetings, he had yet to take one practical step toward true change. The more excuses he made, the more frustrated I became—until I remembered that Herman was a general contractor. I interrupted him mid-story and asked, "Herman, do you have a hammer in your truck?" He did. "Go get it."

When he returned I said, "Herman, every week when we meet, you tell me how bad your problems are, but you won't take any steps toward change. You're like a man who keeps hitting his hand with a hammer, and then comes to me for ice and band-aids. I wrap you up and reduce the swelling, but once you feel better, you leave and hit your hand again. When we see each other next, you tell me how much worse your pain is, and ask for more ice and band-aids. I am glad to give you ice and band-aids, but you need to stop hitting your hand with the hammer, spiritually speaking. At first, I thought you were hitting your hand because you've been aiming for the nail and missing. Now I realize that you're actually hitting your hand on purpose. These are self-inflicted wounds. I cannot help you unless you are willing to give me the hammer."

Herman stormed out. Now he had pastor problems. A couple weeks went by, then he pulled up in his truck again. Red-faced, he burst into my office with news of how his life had worsened since we had last met, and how he needed my support more than ever. I listened for a short bit, then interrupted him, saying, "Herman, are you ready to give me the hammer?"

He knew what I meant. I wanted to know if he was willing to take personal responsibility and do his part in the change process. Taken back by my effort to cut to the chase, he looked me in the face and blurted out a stern "No!" Then he stormed away. This happened a few more times, with each episode getting shorter and shorter. Finally, Herman came into my office one day with a real hammer that had his name on it, and he laid it down in surrender. He gave it to me. Do you know what happened next? He started to change, and then to heal. I can work with that all day, as long as he leaves the hammer alone. He learned that faithful and able was a better plan.

You might have to get to that point when you are mentoring someone. You might need a way to find out whether the guy you're discipling is serious about change. That doesn't mean you should make him meet you at the local cross-fit gym at 4:00 a.m. and flip tires for an hour or hold a five-minute plank, but it's legit to look for proof that the guy you're thinking about discipling has some skin in the game.

Timothy was faithful and able. We can see why Paul chose him. Paul knew that investing in Timothy would be worthwhile. Read again about the day Paul enlisted him as a relatively new believer:

> Paul came also to Derbe and to Lystra. A disciple was there, named Timothy, the son of a Jewish woman who was a believer, but his father was a Greek. He was well spoken of by the brothers at Lystra and Iconium. Paul wanted Timothy to accompany him, and he took him and circumcised him because of the Jews who were in those places, for they all knew that his father was a Greek. As they went on their way through the cities, they delivered to them for observance the decisions that had been reached by the apostles and elders who were in Jerusalem. So the churches were strengthened in the faith, and they increased in numbers daily (Acts 16:1-5).

Lystra is the place where Paul was stoned and left for dead during his first missionary journey. God was so much at work that Paul refused to be pushed out. After Paul left, he couldn't wait to get back. On that return visit, Paul found Timothy, who was already growing at such a rapid rate that "he was well spoken of" by everyone there. He was faithful. Paul was looking for someone who was serious about his spiritual growth—so serious that it was obvious to everyone. Timothy was a standout, a spiritual first-round draft pick. The pace at which he had grown, the evidence of genuine fruit, the reputation for godliness among other believers—all of that magnetized Paul to Timothy. Paul really wanted Timothy to accompany him on the journey.

But notice as well that Timothy made himself available. He *wanted* to be discipled. We don't know what was said in the initial conversations between the two, or how long Paul waited before choosing Timothy, but there's no record of hesitation in the latter. He didn't have to be coaxed from behind his mother's apron. He just upped and left with Paul. And as they went, Paul entrusted Timothy with a measure of responsibility. Timothy dove right in and did it with competency. This example tells us to find men who aren't wishy-washy or flakey. Single out those who are willing to be stretched beyond their comfort zone and give up the familiar. Call men to step up and step out. That's faithful and able.

Timothy also paid the price. Living in Lystra allowed this young Christian to experience the cost of discipleship. Being a Christian could get you killed, especially if you were with Paul. But Timothy had seen his mentor filled with God, truth, and courage. This showed him how to have confidence, even in the face of death. He knew joining Paul wasn't like signing up for a time-share. It was more like training for the Army's Delta Force. Even so, I'm sure he did a double take and asked for clarification when Paul "took him and circumcised him" (Acts 16:3). Ouch! Talk about taking one for the team! It's one thing when you're eight days old, the traditional age for circumcision, but quite another in your twenties or thirties.

I am glad this passage is *description* rather than *prescription* when it comes to discipleship. At stake here was a bigger principle, a kingdom priority. With circumcision, Paul was asking Timothy to remove any unnecessary barriers to the gospel. The Jews would see circumcision as a deal breaker. They would never listen to the gospel if Timothy remained as he was. It had to be done to take away their objections, and just like that, it was.

Difficulties would intensify over time. Regularly, Timothy would face "take-a-deep-breath, swallow-hard, here-we-go" kinds of encounters. But never did he flinch or desert Paul. Sure, he was prone to be timid, but wouldn't you be if you had to weather the storms of ministry with Paul? Yes, you would.

I also find it important to note that Paul was the initiator in the discipling relationship. "Paul wanted Timothy to accompany him, and he took him" (verse 3). That seems to be the biblical pattern—the discipler pursues the disciple. It's how Jesus did it too. When you see someone who exhibits the kinds of qualities Timothy had, don't hesitate. Make the first move.

Question 2: What should you pour into the person you disciple?

If you are going to invest the calories into your Timothy, you should have a good idea of what to give him. I believe this is where most discipling relationships fizzle out. Both mentors and disciples can have good intent, but a lack of clarity can lead to frustration. If you don't know, he won't know. You guys might spend time together, but if you don't know what you're doing, he is likely to move on. Who could blame him?

What do you do when someone says yes to Jesus and wants to grow? Read a systematic theology book together? Download a Puritan paperback and talk about it at the local coffee shop? Pretend you're the Bible Answer Man and attempt to field all the questions he throws at you? Take him wherever you go?

Let's look again at what Paul said in 2 Timothy 2:2. He told Timothy to impart "what you have heard from me in the presence of many witnesses." So, pass on everything that your mentor has given you. Paul took what he got from Jesus, and gave it all to Timothy. Looking closer, Paul wanted Timothy to think about those moments when he taught "in the presence of many witnesses." This can only refer to divinely inspired truth, publicly proclaimed and personally modeled.

But that still begs the question about specifics. Everything Jesus taught encapsulates both the Old and New Testaments. Do we just open the Bible and pick a place at random? It seems popular to start with the Gospel of John, but is that the best thing to do? Are there categories of doctrines and practices that should be in every discipling relationship? What should be our starting point? Thankfully the Bible provides one! Scripture tells us what to give every believer at every stage of spiritual growth. The answer is in 1 John. Under inspiration, Jesus's earthly best friend described the journey from spiritual infancy to fatherhood:

> I am writing to you, little children, because your sins are forgiven for his name's sake. I am writing to you, fathers, because you know him who is from the beginning. I am writing to you, young men, because you have overcome the evil one. I write to you, children, because you know the Father. I write to you, fathers, because you know him who is from the beginning. I write to you, young men, because you are strong, and the word of God abides in you, and you have overcome the evil one (1 John 2:12-14).

> Little children, keep yourselves from idols (5:21).

John identifies three stages of spiritual growth in terms we all understand. He classifies us as either little children, young men, or fathers. Each of these stages has a specific benchmark of growth, which helps takes the guesswork out of mentoring. It tells you what to do, and when. You can find evidences of these benchmarks in Paul's relationship with Timothy. Here's what you are to pour into your disciple so that he is firmly rooted:

Assurance of Salvation—Teach Him to Rest in His Security

John wrote, "I am writing to you, little children, because your sins are forgiven for his name's sake" (2:12). The first thing a new believer should understand is that though he is in Christ, he still sins. But the Savior who saved him still holds and keeps him. All his sins are forgiven: past, present, and future. He no longer stands guilty before God the Judge. He is eternally inseparable from God the Father, through Jesus Christ.

I know you know how important this is. Think about when you first became saved. How many times did you "pray the prayer" again or ask God to save you just in case the first time it didn't take or it wasn't real? Why did you do that? Because you had a hard time understanding how you could be a Christian yet still struggle with sin. That's why assurance of salvation is so important. All of us, and especially brand new believers, need this assurance.

Assurance is the confidence that your salvation is genuine. It's knowing that yes, you are God's own, and that nothing can take that away (see John 10:27-30; 1 Peter 1:3-5). Assurance is also a powerful motivator for holiness (Romans 8:12-17). For your disciple, this assurance will prove helpful in certain seasons of life. In suffering, he will come to you confessing that he has said and done things he never thought a Christian could, like when Peter denied Christ (1 Peter 1:6-9; see also Luke 22:54-62). After giving in to temptation, he will wonder about his standing before God, and you need to teach him the war cry of Paul, who saw himself as a "wretched man" but for whom "there is no condemnation" (Romans 7:14–8:1). When fear sets in, your disciple might waver in doubt because his expectations about Christ go unmet, like they did for John the Baptist, who wondered whether Jesus was even the Christ (Luke 7:18-28). Even strong men struggle, and that's okay.

When that happens to your disciple, as it does to each of us, teach him to anchor his hope in Christ's work for him and in him. Help him to stop measuring his performance and instead rehearse the promises of God. Teach him specific Bible verses like Philippians 1:6, 2 Timothy 2:13, and Jude 24-25. When he finds scriptures that seem to suggest he can lose his salvation (Hebrews 6:4-6), help him to interpret them in light of clearer ones (1 John 2:19). The assurance he gains will allow him to go after Christ without distraction.

Intimacy with God—Invite Him to Enjoy the Father's Heart

When God designed salvation, He did it in a way that we would understand our relationship to Him as a child to a Father. Unlike man-made religions, we don't behave to earn the favor of a deity. Only in Christianity do we learn to love and enjoy the God who made us. John continued, "I am writing to you, fathers, because you know him who is from the beginning…I write to you, children, because you know the Father" (1 John 2:13).

Did you notice the amazing difference between spiritual children and spiritual fathers who have walked with God for a long time? There's none. Both children and fathers "know" Him—a word that refers to relational, not head knowledge. They both know Him, but the spiritual father has persevered in his relationship with God without tiring of Him. The young believer is just at the beginning of that journey. It is here that we gain a profound insight into the mentoring process: You will know you are helping someone grow when he refuses to let his closeness with God drift or grow cold.

In John 4:21-23, knowing the Father means becoming a worshipper who is free from worthless pursuits. This means you help your disciple flee worldliness. In Galatians 4:4-7, it's teaching him to give in to those Spirit-prompted, internal longings to enjoy the

Father devotionally. In Ephesians 1:5, it's reminding him that as an adopted child of God, he will experience greater intimacy with the Father as he cultivates a greater intensity of holiness (Romans 8:12-17). Essentially, you are inviting your disciple to trust that everything that happens in life, including his trials, is an expression of the Father's love, and therefore is an opportunity to be made more like Christ (Romans 8:28-29). As a mentor, you are giving him the gift of an entirely new motivation for living.

Victory over Satan—Urge Him to Say No to Temptation

John goes on, "I am writing to you, young men, because you have overcome the evil one...I write to you, young men, because you are strong, and the word of God abides in you, and you have overcome the evil one" (1 John 2:13-14). Twice John says the mark of a Christian who is growing from spiritual infancy toward maturity is his victory over "the evil one." Your disciple has reached spiritual adulthood when he is defeating the lies, temptations, and tactics of Satan.

Remember this: Satan hates you, hates your disciple, hates your mentoring process, and wants to cause as much disruption to your disciple's growth as possible. The more your Timothy grows, the more vital it will be to equip him with the spiritual armor of Ephesians 6:10-18. Suffice it to say, Satan has two main weapons that work on believers: false teaching and temptation. If he can get your disciple to stop listening to Scripture or lure him away from obedience to God, he can wreak havoc. That's why you must turn your Timothy's heart to the one who overcame the enemy and lives in us who believe.

Your disciple should be aware that Satan never sleeps and that temptation is always coming (Matthew 4:1-2). Your disciple doesn't have to seek temptation—Satan will bring it to him. It will happen when he's most isolated from others and most vulnerable in weakness. You will need to help your disciple identify what his weak areas are. Make it clear to your Timothy that with God's help, he can resist the devil (James 4:7). But don't let him underestimate Satan's pull, which will always come from one of three different directions: the lust of the flesh, the lust of the eyes, and the pride of life (1 John 2:16). When tempted, he will want bodily gratification, visual stimulation, or personal exaltation, but he must learn to resist (Matthew 4:3-10). All sins falls into one of these three categories. But your disciple can be victorious if he remembers God's Word, trusts God's character, and submits to God's plan. When he overcomes, his victory will make him ready for when "the evil one" returns (see Luke 4:13).

Those whom I disciple are given permission to call me anytime, day or night, if they are under the intense pressure of temptation. It might be the temptation of a heated argument with a spouse, the intense pull to reach for a bottle or needle, or the siren call of Internet pornography. If the enemy has my Timothy on the ropes, it doesn't matter if it's 3:00 a.m. If he feels he is about to go down, I want him to get me out of bed rather than dishonor Jesus Christ. I will talk with him, pray with him, rehearse Scripture to him, and if needed, drive to where he is and help him. As a mentor, I believe it's my job to give this lifeline and accountability. I don't want to hear about it a week later.

By the way, I believe a disciple's unwillingness to take a lifeline reveals something about his heart's loyalty to protect a sin. If he gives in to temptation and my phone doesn't ring, this becomes a deal-breaker for the mentoring relationship. We cannot afford to play patty-cake with Satan.

Knowledge of Scripture—Expect Him to Feed Himself on Truth

Another mark of spiritual young adulthood, according to John, is a dynamic relationship with the Word of God. "I write to you, young men, because you are strong, and the word of God abides in you" (1 John 2:14). God has tied His power to His Word (2 Peter 1:3-4), which offers everything we as believers need for life and godliness. Without it, we cannot be holy (John 17:17).

One habit I have cultivated with my son since he was five is to study the book of Proverbs together with him. In Bible times, kids were supposed to have chapters 1–9 mastered by puberty (I got a late start). Proverbs is the most practical book in the Bible, filled with specifics on how to honor God in every situation. Typically on my days off or on Saturday mornings, I wake up Ty early and we head to the nearest donut shop with a Bible, journal, pen, and a few bucks. We started with the cast of characters: the wise man, the fool, the prudent, the naive, the wicked, the scoffer, the sluggard, and the harlot, as well as verses like "The fear of the LORD is the beginning of wisdom" (9:10). Even before he could read or write, I would read specific proverbs to him and lead a discussion about different scenarios he would face where that truth would spare him from sin's consequences, while he drew a picture of the concept as he munched on chocolate-glazed donuts. Ty knows how to avoid the seductive woman, how to use his money, what to look for in a real friend, how to work hard, be generous, honor others, and live his life in the conscious presence of the God he loves and fears disappointing. My goal is that when he turns 18 and leaves our home, he will have a head full of truth that entered his ears when he was little and made the 18-inch trek to his heart.

Our job as mentors to show our mentees how Scripture is profitable in everyday life (2 Timothy 3:16-17)—in decisions, relationships, and problem-solving. They should see us speak of God's Word as unerring in what it says (Psalm 119:160), trust it as unfailing in what it promises (Joshua 23:14), obey it as authoritative in all it commands (Titus 2:1,15), and sufficient when the world offers us a different wisdom (Psalm 19:7-9).

Don't be alarmed if your mentee gets overwhelmed. The Bible is not one book, but 66 ancient books, each with its own author, literary genre, and purpose. Some of it will be hard for him to understand (2 Peter 3:15-16). But the same Holy Spirit who wrote it will open his heart to understand and welcome it (1 Corinthians 2:14-16). Keep him reading (Psalm 1:1-3), studying (2 Timothy 2:15), memorizing (Colossians 3:16), meditating (Joshua 1:8), and applying (James 1:19-27). There should never be an occasion where you don't speak or model God's Word to him.

Defense Against Idolatry—Warn Him to Run Away from Danger

John closes his epistle with a warning to new Christians: "Little children, keep yourselves from idols" (1 John 5:21). With one final exhortation, he warns new believers to stay away from those things that take God's place in our hearts and affections. Often associated with statues in the Old Testament, idolatry was the way people created a god of their liking. They did this because the true, living God was an obstacle to their desires. Sometimes they changed their view of the true God to make Him more manageable. Other times they rejected Him outright and invented a new deity altogether. In simple terms, idols are man-made replacements for God.

I experienced the reality of idolatry when I was in Pune, India.

I was approached by a young woman who attended the gathering we were hosting. She wanted to ask me questions about the Creator God of the Bible. She had become dissatisfied with idolatry and the enslavement to the 110 different gods her family worshipped. At the top of the idol pyramid in her home was the Hindu god Ganesh—the exalted elephant boy who rode in the heavens on a rat. As one version of the story goes, Ganesh was a young boy-god who wandered into his divine parents' bedroom one day when he should have knocked, and saw them in a compromising position. In embarrassed fear, he ran out of the house and into the forest with his angry god-father Shiva chasing him. When the dad finally caught up with him, he decapitated his boy. The god-mother, in a frenzy and panic, summoned the animals of the forest together and asked if any of them were willing to give up their head so that the boy might live. Bravely, the elephant stepped forward to tender his noggin, and Ganesh was saved (and elephants were forever elevated). Now this part-boy, part-elephant parades throughout the heavens, granting wishes and removing obstacles on behalf of his devoted followers.

The young woman then explained that when she adorned the statue, put plates of food before him, shrouded the carving with flowers, and lit candles that sparkled off his polished zinc and embedded jewels, she was trying to get his attention so that he would give her what she wanted. She was manipulating the deity, who wanted recognition among the other gods, and leveraging that for her own advantage. In her prayers, she threatened the deity that if he didn't come through on her wish, she would forsake him and devote herself to another. She came to me confessing that she knew there was only one God—the God who made the universe, and she wanted to know His name. I told her, "His name is Jesus."

Now, while we might shake our heads over the fact people

actually believe that kind of stuff, we are just as guilt of idolatry when we try to domesticate the one true God and manipulate Him for our own benefit. Sometimes our wants come into conflict with what we know to be true about God, and we allow ourselves to be enslaved when He has offered us true freedom. We too have been guilty of slacking off in our commitment to Him when He doesn't give us the life we want. Our idols are our desires, and if we are honest, we have to admit that we often give greater priority to our desires than we do to God.

Idols are forbidden by God. He is jealous for His glory and for us (Exodus 20:4-5; see also Zechariah 8:2). We can help our followers identify idolatry when they hear themselves saying things like, "I need this to be happy!" "I will sin to get it, or sin if I don't get it!" These heart idols must be torn down (Proverbs 4:23; Ezekiel 14:1-11). Disciples need to see that idols never satisfy. They only disappoint and enslave (Jeremiah 2:9-13; Isaiah 46:5-7). Those who make room for idols will come to ruin (1 Kings 11:1-12,14,23,27, 42-43). No wonder true salvation is described as turning away from idols (1 Thessalonians 1:9; see also Ezekiel 36:25).

If your Timothy feels his heart drifting, chances are that an idol is leading him astray. If he finds himself without the strength of God, help him search for hidden idolatry (Jonah 2:8). Help him take aggressive measures to not allow any form of idolatry into his home (Deuteronomy 7:26). Push him to scan his friendships and flee those that are influencing him toward idolatry of one kind or another (Psalms 26:5; 31:6). And if he should risk losing everything to be free of idolatry, remind him that the one true God stands with him (see Daniel 3:18-30).

What could your Timothy's life look like if he was rooted and grounded, with a life defined by these benchmarks? Can you think of anything that's missing? Anything else you could ever impart can be built on this foundation.

Question 3: How will you benefit personally from having a disciple?

By now it should be obvious that it's not wise to enter into a mentoring relationship if you're not serious about what it requires. At the same time, I hope I've made it clear that being a mentor has great benefit to you. Discipling relationships allow you to gain personally from the men you mentor. The more you put in, the more you get out. Yes, the mentee comes under you, but it's not all one-sided. He takes from you, but he also adds to you. You benefit in three major ways:

Discipleship Doubles the Workforce and Lightens Your Load

Discipleship is duplication. That's why Paul said, "Be imitators of me, as I am of Christ" (1 Corinthians 11:1). It allows us to reproduce ourselves in the lives of those we disciple. No doubt this is the reason Jesus warned us to be careful who we let into our lives. In Luke 6:39-40, He said, "Can a blind man lead a blind man? Will they not both fall into a pit? A disciple is not above his teacher, but everyone when he is fully trained will be like his teacher."

If done right, your disciple will carry some of your load, which, in turn, will allow you to focus more on the other things you are called to do. Can you imagine a race car driver pulling into the pit, unbuckling his harness, hopping out of the car, getting the jack, dragging the jack over to the car, lining it up in the right position, and pumping up the car so the tire guys can put on new wheels? Then when the tire guys are done, he puts the jack back where it

Discipling relationships allow
you to gain personally from
the men you mentor.
**The more you put in,
the more you get out.**
Yes, the mentee comes
under you, but it's not all
one-sided. He takes from you,
but he also adds to you.

belongs, climbs into his car, buckles up again, and speeds off into the race. Doing all that would be both distracting and exhausting. The jack-man not only saves the driver precious seconds, he keeps him focused on driving and winning.

Once you have found someone who meets the criteria of faithful and able, follow this time-tested pattern. Say to your Timothy:

"I'll do, and you watch."

Here's the first step in passing the baton. Paul didn't throw the baton at Timothy and tell him to run with it. He gave him a clear example of how to hold the baton and run with it without dropping it. Then he put the baton in Timothy's hand and showed him how to hold it.

On the second missionary journey, while Paul and Silas were in the fray, Timothy was an observer. He was detached enough that he escaped imprisonment, but close enough to see faithfulness in suffering. This would prove helpful later when Timothy read these words: "Share in suffering as a good soldier of Christ Jesus" (2 Timothy 2:3). Letting Timothy experience the work of ministry firsthand was a vital part of explaining it. Don't just tell him, show him.

"I'll do, and you help."

It's life-giving when you have someone you can give an assignment to without having to hold his hand. He might not be able to handle the whole project himself, but you can transfer some weight to him. His contribution will be enough to be a real help. You're not just "throwing him a bone."

Later during the second missionary trip, Timothy helped Paul to establish a church and then went back to do some follow-up work. Paul called Timothy "our brother and God's coworker in the gospel"

(1 Thessalonians 3:2). He also called Timothy one of his "helpers" in Acts 19:22. This illustrates there is going to come a time when you must give your disciple a real assignment. You're going to have to know the right time and setting, and make sure he is prepared for the task. He needs to know his role and how to measure whether he's done the job well. Make sure you let him in on the plans and give him access to your resources. Platform him with the other workers, tell him the timeline, and show him how his tools should be used. But be careful to give him a responsibility that both utilizes him and stretches him. This can sometimes be a hard balance to discern. If you put him in the kiddie pool wearing arm floaties, you will humiliate him. If you push him into the deep end of the pool too soon, you'll become the lifeguard and he will struggle to trust you.

"You do, and I'll help."

This was Timothy when he was sent out to the deeply troubled church of Corinth. As he went, Paul helped by telling the church members, "I sent you Timothy, my beloved and faithful child in the Lord, to remind you of my ways in Christ, as I teach them everywhere in every church" (1 Corinthians 4:17). Later in the same letter, Paul helped again with this statement: "When Timothy comes, see that you put him at ease among you, for he is doing the work of the Lord, as I am" (16:10). This tells us that Timothy was mature enough to do more than watch and help. He was ready to lead, such that Paul didn't even need to go at all. Paul still offered help through his epistle, but because Timothy was present, Paul could stay focused in Ephesus (1 Corinthians 16:8-9).

This shift was seismic. Here the disciple traded places with the mentor. This particular assignment wasn't for the faint of heart. Corinth was a distressing church. The people there would have eaten a younger Timothy alive. But he had reached the point where he was able to step into the fray and Paul could coach from a distance. When your disciple gets to this point, you begin to experience the benefits of discipleship. He does what you would do, says what you would say, reacts like you would react. He still needs you, but it's only for encouragement and reinforcement, not course correction. Then he's ready to lead without you.

"You do, and I'll watch."

This was Timothy at the end of Paul's life in 2 Timothy 4, when the apostle pleaded with him to come quickly to him in prison. Paul knew that he was about to die as a martyr, and that he was totally vulnerable. Timothy was not used to seeing Paul in this position. The once-timid disciple would see his mentor go off the scene as he took up the mantle and carried on the work. While the enormity of this transition certainly would have jarred and even frightened Timothy, Paul knew he was ready. He would have to be. When you reach this point with your disciple, you can deploy and enjoy him. Then you can begin again with someone else.

This is how discipleship works. It is not a sit-down-over-coffee-and-tell-me-about-your-struggles-and-I-will-give-you-Bible-verses kind of thing. It's a dynamic, in-motion, kingdom-shouldering, working-together relationship built on a foundation of love and loyalty, to Christ and to each other. This kind of relationship is powerful when done right, and is rare indeed. It also builds a sweet bond like no other.

Discipleship Provides the Deepest and Dearest of Bonds

Mentoring is deeply personal, as it should be. Just a cursory reading of Paul's letters tells you of the affection Paul shared with Timothy.

He wrote, "To Timothy, my true child in the faith…" (1 Timothy 1:2). "This charge I entrust to you, Timothy, my child…" (1 Timothy 1:18). "To Timothy, my beloved child: Grace, mercy, and peace from God the Father and Christ Jesus our Lord" (2 Timothy 1:2).

Paul speaks of Timothy in the most endearing way—as a father to his son. Timothy would have been valuable to Paul, who was single and had no children that we know of. In the same way, Paul would have been precious to Timothy, whose biological father had not invested in him spiritually.

It could also be that Paul had more in mind. In the ancient world, Roman fathers adopted sons as their own when they were already grown. It was unlike our day, where parents adopt kids as early as possible. In Paul's day, adoption happened when fathers did not have an heir, or an heir they believed would carry on the family legacy in honor. Thus they would select a young man who was in his twenties or thirties and ask him to become a son. Once confirmed legally, the adopted son would carry the full weight of actual sonship. In most cases, he would have a greater claim to the inheritance left by the father than natural-born children. And unlike biological children, this adopted son could never be disowned. He would carry forth the legacy and honor of his father.

Could this be what Paul had in mind? If so, he adopted Timothy in a spiritual sense and willed the legacy of gospel ministry to him. This would have provided Paul with an heir of sorts—someone to carry on the ministry after he was gone.

Discipleship Ensures the Longevity of Your Vision and Legacy

Perhaps most satisfying aspect of discipleship is that it allows you to have a long-term impact. People you've never met and generations yet to be born will be affected by your life. If you make disciples who make disciples who make disciples, you can disciple generations of people by pouring your life into one person. In turn, those disciples will reach others in places you've never been to.

Also, those you mentor not only grow and help others, they pick up where you left off and go further. And if you think about it, if you start early as a mentor, those whom you train up can actually grow to be further along than you are by the time they reach your age. I started Ty on a very intentional process of discipleship when he was five. My mentor started on me at 18. By the time my son gets to 18, he will be light-years ahead of where I was with so much less baggage than I had. When he gets to 43, he will likely have progressed beyond what I might reach in a lifetime. And think about what will happen in the lives of the men he mentors, when he takes what he's learned and gives it away.

If you will commit to the discipleship process, the legacy of Christianity will strengthen rather than weaken. And your eternal rewards will multiply exponentially as your influence spreads through the lives of others.

The Goal of Mentoring Is God

When Timothy read Paul's last letter, he learned that Paul was going to die a martyr's death. Their mentoring relationship was about to end. He might not ever see Paul again this side of heaven. But Paul could sign off with confidence about Timothy because his confidence was never in Timothy. It was in the Lord. God would take Paul's place. Paul had pointed Timothy to God.

The most valuable lesson in discipleship is this: The goal of mentoring is God. When you read 2 Timothy, you see at critical points how Paul layered in truths about God, which Timothy would need going forward. Timothy still had issues to work through, and Paul was forthright about them. But more than a list of duties, Paul's last letter reminded Timothy about God. In fact, he had done that his entire ministry.

In the long run, you're not teaching your Timothy to depend on you or be like you. You're teaching your Timothy to depend on God and be like God. When you do that, and when that relationship is over, the true Discipler takes over and does His perfect work.

What happened to Timothy? The only time his name appeared again after Paul's death is in the book of Hebrews—a letter about suffering. After urging his readers to cling to Christ amid horrific persecution, the author gives the example of Timothy: "You should know that our brother Timothy has been released, with whom I shall see you if he comes soon" (Hebrews 13:23).

Timothy had been imprisoned, but he stood for the faith. In a hostile environment, much like that which Paul faced, Timothy fared well without his mentor and became the leader of the church. Why was this once thin-skinned, timid, inadequate, overwhelmed young man able to do it? Because he had a mentor? Yes, but more so because he had his mentor's God.

Do you want to leave a lasting mark? Be a mentor—one who trains up those who are faithful and able and points them to God.

Important Takeaways to Remember

- All we have to do is nothing, and all that has been entrusted to us will die with us.
- Disciple men who are faithful and able.
- Don't waste your time pouring into men who are not "faithful and able." Like a man who smashes his hand with a hammer on purpose, they will only inflict themselves further if they do not listen to your counsel. Invest in those who are willing to hand you the hammer.
- Mentoring means you have a plan to help your disciple grow. If you don't have a plan, your intentions might be good, but your disciple won't stick around.
- Help the one you mentor lay the following five foundation stones:
  1. Assurance of salvation
  2. Intimacy with God
  3. Victory over Satan
  4. Knowledge of Scripture
  5. Defense against idolatry
- Offer your disciple a lifeline for temptation, by which he can contact you when the enemy has him on the ropes.
- Passing on responsibility to a disciple is done in four important, easy to remember steps: I'll do and you watch; I'll do and you help; you do and I'll help; you do and I'll watch.
- The goal of mentoring is God.

Finding Your Timothy

Jesus called us to fulfill His mission by discipling others. Hopefully you strive to be the kind of man whom others desire to emulate. The questions below are designed to stimulate your own growth as a mentor. They are also here to help you find the kind of disciple who is best suited to learn from you. It's possible that in this process, you will see some areas in your own life that you can take to the next level. As a discipler, you'll want to "up your game" and become more intentional about helping others follow you as you follow Christ.

1. As you think through Paul's criteria for discipleship and the men in your life, which of them would make the best candidate as your Timothy? Write down their names, and the qualities they exhibit.

2. As you consider what a mentor pours into his disciple, are you reminded of areas in your own life that need strengthening? Write them below. Let the call to disciple others offer you the opportunity to grow as well. Expand your study of the spiritual benchmarks listed in 1 John 2:12-14; 5:21 and described in this chapter. Make sure you are refreshing your own walk with Christ. You can't give it if you don't have it.

3. Different people learn in different ways. Some people learn as they read and analyze, while others grasp as they talk and listen. Some are wired to absorb by wrestling through problems and solving them, while others are hands-on and learn by doing. Which way do you learn? Which way does your disciple learn? If your disciple learns in a different way than you, that's okay—you just need to know how to guide him. Record your thoughts below.

4. In this chapter, we learned that the goal of mentoring is God. Grab a highlighter and read about the character of God in 1 and 2 Timothy. Mark every reference Paul makes to an attribute of God and how it motivates Timothy to act on Paul's instruction. What did Paul teach his disciple about the person of God?

CHAPTER 6

You Need a Lost Seeker to Hear You

The most perfect person to ever walk on earth was Jesus, yet He is one of the most hated men in history. That is strange, because He is the model for everything good, right, and holy. Among all the things He did for us, He showed what it is like to be a man, the way God intended. He took on human nature and showed us how to live it. No matter what people thought of Him, everyone wanted to be near Him and stay near Him, though not for the same reasons. His followers never left Him alone, and His enemies loomed within earshot to hear what He would say and see what He would do.

Lepers violated city codes to be cleansed by Him. Large masses stepped on each other to get a glimpse of Him. Children lined up like kids at Macy's during Christmas to sit on His lap. Multitudes sat for hours on the mountainside to listen to Him expound Scripture in the blazing sun. A group of men tore pieces from a roof to get their paralyzed friend closer to Him. Prostitutes interrupted His dinners to pour out gratitude on Him. Tax collectors threw parties for Him and spent hours eating and drinking with Him.

Everyone wanted a piece of Jesus—everyone, that is, except the religious leaders. They hated Him. Odd that God the Son was despised most by religious people. They had many colorful names for Him, including Beelzebul (means lord of the flies that hover over dung), glutton, and drunkard. One of the nicknames they came up with was "friend of…sinners" (Luke 7:34).

To them, this title meant He was full of compromise. But to us, it reminds us that He was full of mercy. It was a label He was glad to wear, which was good news to those who knew they were sinners.

Because Jesus was the friend of sinners, our conversation about guy friends should include the friends in our lives who need Jesus. Take a second and write the names of five men in the margin of this page. Do it right now.

Jesus had many friends like yours. One of the most familiar to us is one whom most kids learn about in children's church. It's the story of that "wee little man" who "climbed up in the sycamore tree, for the Lord he wanted to see."

He was lost, but he was a seeker. His name was Zacchaeus. And he was exactly the kind of guy God has in your life—someone who needs salvation. He's the person for whom God wants you to stop everything, important as it may be, so you can tell him the good news of salvation.

Luke tells the story like this:

> He entered Jericho and was passing through. And behold, there was a man named Zacchaeus. He was a chief tax collector and was rich. And he was seeking to see who Jesus was, but on account of the crowd he could not, because he was small in stature. So he ran on ahead and climbed up

into a sycamore tree to see him, for he was about to pass
that way. And when Jesus came to the place, he looked up
and said to him, "Zacchaeus, hurry and come down, for
I must stay at your house today." So he hurried and came
down and received him joyfully. And when they saw it,
they all grumbled, "He has gone in to be the guest of a man
who is a sinner." And Zacchaeus stood and said to the Lord,
"Behold, Lord, the half of my goods I give to the poor. And
if I have defrauded anyone of anything, I restore it fourfold." And Jesus said to him, "Today salvation has come to
this house, since he also is a son of Abraham. For the Son
of Man came to seek and to save the lost" (Luke 19:1-10).

The key to understanding this story is the last sentence: "For
the Son of Man came to seek and to save the lost." Here, Jesus
verbalized His own personal mission statement: to seek and save
sinners.

The name *Zacchaeus* is Jewish and means "pure one," but this
man was anything but pure or Jewish. He was the chief tax collector in Jericho. To Jews, tax collectors were the worst of sinners. They
worked for the pagan government of Rome, who suppressed Israel.
This meant the tax gatherers were more than an ancient IRS. They
had a greater allegiance to Caesar and to their own wallets than to
their own people. Greater than their brothers and sisters or their heritage of faith. To make a living as a tax collector, simply put, you collected taxes for Rome. But the reason tax collectors were so despised
is that Rome allowed them to take whatever *else* they wanted as they
collected taxes. That made Zacchaeus a thief and a traitor.

Jericho was also one of the best places for a tax collector to get
rich. It was a lush oasis, rich with expensive goods. It was given the
names "the paradise of God" and the "city of roses" because of its
beauty. It had roads lined with palm and sycamore trees. Think

Beverly Hills. Moreover, it was a major crossroad, making it a trade city. This meant more opportunities for taxation, which, in turn, meant more money in Zacchaeus's pockets. And worse still, he was the "chief" tax collector. This guy was at the top of the pyramid.

Zacchaeus gave everyone instant acid reflux. He was the ultimate bad guy: He was indulgent and engaged in extortion, apostasy, and betrayal. Perfect! Just the kind of sinner Jesus loves to save. This is why He came. In John 3:17 we read, "God did not send his Son into the world to condemn the world, but in order that the world might be saved through him." Jesus reminded His disciples in Luke 9:56, "The Son of Man did not come to destroy men's lives, but to save them" (NASB).

Strategies from the Heart of Christ

David Livingstone said, "God had only one Son, and He was a missionary."[4] True that. Let's watch Him work and follow His example as He models five strategies that we can use to bring our friends to Christ. And remember, as is always true of Jesus, we are not merely looking at strategies, we are looking at His heart. My aim is to stir you up to have the kind of heart Spurgeon described, "Soul winning must be your passion, you must be born to it; it must be the very breath of your nostrils, the only thing for which you count life worth having."[5] Here's how:

Strategy #1: Put Yourself Where They Are

It's critical to note where Jesus was at this point in His life. According to the chronology, Jesus was at the dead end of His three-and-a-half-year ministry, literally. He was only days away from the cross. It's also been a year since He has been out of the public eye, during which time He prepared the apostles for His departure. Missing in action on purpose. He knew where the hate would lead—Golgotha.

On occasion, Jesus's paparazzi would spot Him and spread the word of His whereabouts. As quickly as possible, He would slip back into hiding. Only a few days before His encounter with Zacchaeus, He did His most astonishing miracle to date. He raised a man from the dead—a man who had already been in heaven four days. This created a fever pitch of frenetic activity that caused the nation to start buzzing again. Jesus was back. Added to that, everyone learned He was coming to the feast of Passover in Jerusalem. It was as if He was stepping onto the red carpet and flashbulbs were going crazy.

What no one knew was that His ministry was over. Jesus was done. The cross was all that remained. The religious leaders were about to kill Him. But He took this Jericho road and pushed through the sea of onlookers on His way to a divine appointment with a man who needed salvation. There was someone He had come to save, and today was the day.

What's amazing is that Jesus was at this place at this time. He didn't have to be. Jericho wasn't exactly on the route to where He was going. If Siri had been invented, she would have continually muttered, "Proceed to the route…make a U-turn." There were other routes that Jesus could have taken. His face was hardened like flint toward Jerusalem and His mind was on bearing our sin, but He had time for one more sinner.

What's the point? Jesus was where Zacchaeus was. If Zacchaeus was going to be saved, the Savior had to come for him, which meant that Jesus had to put Himself there. Same for us. We have to be where lost people are if we are going to bring them to Christ. We have to seek them out, pursue them, and interact with them. Often we have to go out of our way.

Sadly, many Christians go out of their way to avoid unbelievers. I'm told that one in five people who live in America don't even know one Christian.[6] That's a population roughly the size of greater Los Angeles. How insane! A community the size of one of the world's great alpha cities is completely in the dark, without a gospel witness. Worldwide, it's worse: Eight out of ten people don't have a single believer in his or her life. Not a good statistic for the world's largest religion.

It's easy to get so caught up in our own Christian lives that we forget that Jesus left us on earth to win people for Him. It's the one thing we can't do in heaven. Sometimes we are so busy being "Christian" that we forget to extend that hope to others. We have our Christian churches, Christian schools, Christian clubs, Christian doctors, Christian barbers, Christian mechanics who fix our Christian cars, which we drive listening to our favorite Christian radio stations, commuting to and from our Christian jobs, after which we go to our Christian homes and close our electric Christian fences, and pet our Christian dog, who runs out to protect our Christian families. Everything is so "Christian, Christian, Christian" that we lose contact with the non-Christian world. We are good little Christians without the heart and mission of Christ.

So what should you do? Sell your home, cash out your 401(k), and move to the jungles of Africa? Maybe, but don't go over there to do what you aren't willing to do here. Instead, look in your own locale and read this:

> [God] made from one man every nation of mankind to live on all the face of the earth, having determined allotted periods and the boundaries of their dwelling place, that they should seek God, and perhaps feel their way toward him and find him. Yet he is actually not far from each one of us (Acts 17:26-27).

Have you ever thought about that? Everyone on this planet is exactly where God wants them right now. They were born exactly where and when God wanted them to be born. This is incredible to think about. And they live where they do because God has decided that would be the best place, time, and way for them to seek Him and find Him. It's true for the soldier in war-torn Syria as well as the corn farmer in rural Ohio. It's true for the immigrant fleeing for his life on an inflatable raft to Athens and the kid who grew up in the Bible belt of the South. Everyone is exactly where God wants them because He is orchestrating their lives to either share the gospel or come under the hearing of the gospel. And He has put you in proximity to unsaved people for that purpose.

Mind blown.

Think about how practical this is for the unsaved friends in your life, the five guys you listed earlier. By God's design, you are where they are. God has put you in a web of relationships that have eternal consequence. You walk each day from divine appointment to divine appointment.

Try this: Turn off the talk radio and look at all the people you go by during your commute. They have eternal souls and are going to live forever somewhere—heaven or hell. Walk outside and look down the street you live on—God's wisdom put you on this block. Envision the people who emailed you today, who share the same workplace as you, and who sit in Starbucks while you're there. Picture the guys who load your golf bags for you, who cheer in the stadium with you, who stand in the TSA line with you. Open your smartphone and scroll through the contacts. Do you see what Jesus sees? People for whom He died?

Nothing was so important that Jesus could miss this encounter with Zacchaeus. Not even the cross. So then, with all that we have

By God's design,

you are where they are.

God has put you in a web

of relationships that have

eternal consequence.

You walk each day from

divine appointment to

divine appointment.

on our plates, let's not let neglect this priority. Just look at who God has put around you, and lean into the moment.

Strategy #2: Gauge the Level of Their Interest

God was moving Jesus's feet toward Zacchaeus, and He was moving Zacchaeus's heart toward Jesus. At first, Zacchaeus appeared to be curious about the commotion over the Savior, who no doubt drew all the people away from his tax booth. But this crowd was massive, and Zacchaeus was vertically challenged. As a result, he couldn't see.

Running ahead, Zacchaeus climbed up a sycamore tree to get a better look. The sycamore would have been perfect because its branches hung low, and a little guy could climb up easily and get a great view. At this point, if he had owned an iPhone, he would've posted a selfie. #Jesus

Yet Luke's grammar here tells us that Zacchaeus's desire to see Jesus was actually quite different from that of the rest of the crowd. This was more than a celebrity sighting to him. He was fervently trying to see Jesus. He was studying Him.

We don't know what Zacchaeus knew about the Lord. But given Jesus's fame, it would have been tough to live in Israel at that time and not take in something about Him. For all we know, Zacchaeus had probably taxed Jesus before—Jesus lived there. Whatever Zacchaeus knew, we can be certain that his level of spiritual interest was strong. God was working on his heart. This was Jericho's chief sinner trying harder than anyone to see Christ, and it doesn't require omniscience to see his level of interest.

Did you know that God is working in every single unbelieving human heart right now? He is convicting them that they are sinners, that He is righteous, and that there is a judgment to come (John

16:8). He is drawing some (John 6:44), and hardening others (John 12:36-40). He is interacting meaningfully with everyone at every moment. We might not see it, but it's happening.

Here's what to watch for specifically: Like Zacchaeus, some of our friends show signs of genuine spiritual desire. Their hearts are open to the Bible; they are starting to realize the depth of their sinfulness and feel the emptiness of life in a fallen world. They know that nothing on earth satisfies the soul. They are searching for answers to their deepest needs. In church planting, we teach people to think of outreach like picking apples. Search for the ripe ones because they are ready and will be soft and sweet. By contrast, unripe apples are hard and bitter. Simple strategy, right? If it's ripe, pick it. If it's not, wait until it's ripe, and make sure you don't bruise it in the meantime.

To put it in more theological terms, Scripture says unsaved people do not seek God (Romans 3:10-12). They do not and cannot. If a person is seeking, God must be doing something to get his or her attention. He is stirring that person's heart (see Philippians 1:29; 2 Timothy 2:25). If that's true, we should act because that person is ripe for the gospel.

This doesn't mean we share the good news only with those who want to hear it (Ezekiel 2:7). But we should give priority to those in whose hearts God appears to be working, just as Jesus did. Is that true of any of the guys on your list? Can you think of any one of those five who might be willing to hear about how God saved you?

Strategy #3: Feel the Urgency of Their Need

Five times in one verse, Jesus stressed the urgency of Zacchaeus's need:

- He called him out by name: "Zacchaeus!" This set Zacchaeus apart from the rest of the crowd. It was personal. Jesus stopped what He was doing to address this man, as if to say, "I am talking directly to you!"
- The word "hurry" is a command in the original Greek text and would have added a bit of pressure to the moment. There was no time for delay or hesitation. Move your feet. Go.
- The phrase "come down" was another strong command in the original Greek text. It was used in a tense that emphasizes *do it immediately*! If Jesus had written His words, they would have been in **bold**, *italics*, <u>underlined</u>, and ALL CAPS.
- When? Today! Not tomorrow, next week, or one day in the future when it's convenient. Right now, this instant!
- Finally, Jesus added, "I must stay at your house." Jesus invited Himself to this man's home. This was a bold act. Jesus was graciously intrusive and aggressive.

This was the time. This was the way. Paul wrote about this kind of spiritual gravitas in 2 Corinthians 6:2: "Behold, now is the favorable time; behold, now is the day of salvation." Jesus wasn't rushing because He had to figure out how to squeeze Zacchaeus into His crazy schedule. The urgency was because of what He said in Luke 19:10: He "came to seek and save the lost."

Moreover, the word "lost" goes beyond the idea of a missing person who must be found. It means "to perish, to be destroyed, ruined." The one Jesus sought was done for. He was hopelessly, helplessly lost. His sin had ruined him. He was on his way to hell—forever.

We use the word "lost" in the same way today. When the Nebraska Cornhuskers beat my Florida Gators in 1995 for the NCAA football national championship, at a certain point in the game it became clear to me—and to everyone else watching the game—that it was over (yes, I am still disappointed). There were several minutes left on the clock, but the Gatorade had already stained the winning coach's shirt. The game was beyond salvaging. There was no coming back from this deficit.

The lost must repent and believe the gospel, or they will perish under the wrath of God. Jesus knew this. He felt this. It was why He came, to rescue sinners from perishing. John 3:16: "God so loved the world, that he gave his only Son, that whoever believes in him shall not perish but have eternal life."

So let me ask: What happens in your heart when you think about the lost guys on your list? Do you have the passion of David Brainerd, who said as he was dying, "I cared not where or how I lived, and what hardships I went through, so that I could but gain souls to Christ"?[7] What about Paul, who wrote:

> I am speaking the truth in Christ—I am not lying; my conscience bears me witness in the Holy Spirit—that I have great sorrow and unceasing anguish in my heart. For I could wish that I myself were accursed and cut off from Christ for the sake of my brothers, my kinsmen according to the flesh (Romans 9:1-3).

Read that again: "I could wish that I myself were accursed and cut off from Christ for the sake of my brothers." What? You'd give up your salvation for them? People who hate you and want you dead? Forget about your closest guy friends—these are your enemies! You would take their eternal punishment so they could have your eternal life?

I have to admit I don't love like this. My wife and kids, yes. It's easy to love them. But the guys on my list? Definitely not. I long for their salvation, but not to the point of wanting to give up heaven for them (which is not possible, by the way). Paul wanted that badly for them to be saved. I'm convicted by that. And isn't this exactly what Jesus did for us? He took our eternal punishment so that we could have His eternal life. The heart of Christ in us should cause us to weep and take action.

Strategy #4: Step into the Mess of Their Lives

Notice that Jesus said, "I must stay at your house." The word "stay" means "to remain." Jesus was not stopping by for a few minutes. He was planning to spend a considerable amount of time with Zacchaeus. The Son of Man was not in a hurry; this was why He came.

Have you noticed that whoever was in front of Jesus at any given moment was the most important person in His world? Even the people we tend to treat as if they were invisible or wished would go away. Jesus made room for Himself in Zacchaeus's life and went to where Zacchaeus really lived. This was Zacchaeus's *oikos*—the center of his life, family, job, and entire network of relationships.

I'm sure Zacchaeus didn't get this kind of request often, least of all from a rabbi. Most of the locals would probably rather burn that house down than go into it. An arsonist could have improved the neighborhood and property values would have spiked. But that doesn't make the problem of sin go away. It just moves it to a different location. Too often we act as if to say to unbelievers, "If you want to ruin your life, that's fine—do it somewhere else, away from my family." But Jesus stepped toward Zacchaeus, not away from him.

I love that Zacchaeus "received him joyfully" (Luke 19:6). He wanted time with the Lord too. It was his joy to have the holy God in his house, just as it was Jesus's joy to be there. I don't know if we can adequately feel the emotion of this moment. To even step foot into a tax collector's house was the same as entering a prostitute's house. Doing this was considered "unclean" because of what went on in there.

To the people of that day, when you entered someone's house, you were entering into that person's sphere of life and circle of influence. To many, doing this was an endorsement of the lifestyle of the owner. What's more, to eat with such a person was like having fellowship with darkness. How wrong the religious leaders were! Because of their self-righteousness, they were in the dark too. Their spiritual eyes were blind. And here was the Light of Life at Zacchaeus's door, chasing the darkness away.

This really was a messy situation. Tax collectors were thugs. They were abusive, immoral, gluttonous, and treacherous. Zacchaeus's home was where the prostitutes would have hung out. It was a house furnished by wickedness. But here's the question: Who is going to step into such homes with hope? It's up to us to make the first move. If we don't, who will? Jesus stepped right into the mess. Of course He did.

There is no way to express what a serious taboo this was, especially in Jericho. That city was home to a large number of Jewish priests. So when Jesus prevailed on Zacchaeus to "stay" at his house, He was making a statement to both the sinners and the religious leaders. It is the reason the crowd responded the way they did: "When they saw it, they all grumbled, 'He has gone in to be the guest of a man who is a sinner'" (Luke 19:7).

I can just see Jesus stopping in the midst of this mob and, with a bold, welcoming voice, calling the tax collector's name. I can imagine the crowd turning to follow the line from the Savior's eyes upward to the tree in which Zacchaeus was perched. I am sure emotions were mixed and the tension was high when the people recognized the man who was so hated—so much so that if he were walking down a dark alley at night, he might not make it out alive.

I imagine some people in the crowd expected that Jesus would lay into that lying, thieving, conniving cutthroat. Except He didn't: *"You come down, for I'm going to your house today."* I can picture the crowd parting like the Red Sea to make room for Jesus to walk toward Zacchaeus. To Jesus, Zacchaeus was ripe spiritual fruit hanging from the tree.

Jesus didn't need omniscience to know what the people were murmuring. To the crowd, nothing could be more defiling, disgusting, and double-crossing than to associate with Zacchaeus. This was all that some needed to be done with Jesus for good. Many of them probably headed for home. They had about as much use for Him as a leper. They already didn't want to be near Zacchaeus, and now they didn't want to be near Jesus.

Others in the crowd stayed, knowing the unexpected always happened when Jesus was around. Controversy draws a crowd. And while they were disgusted as well, they kept watching for the sake of the drama, like high schoolers standing around with their cellphones videoing a cafeteria fight.

Some saw this as an opportunity to reject Jesus once and for all, saying things like, "He obviously doesn't know who this man is, or He would not have chosen to go there!" Or, "Of course He knows who this filth is. Didn't you hear the way He called to him? He knows his name. It's like they are friends. He must be one of them." Or maybe, "Once that doors closes, I'll bet the real Jesus is going to come out. The dark side. Have you seen the parties that are thrown in that house? The women! The food! The alcohol! The music!"

"Yep. He's a friend of sinners," someone would have quipped. Jesus would have heard that and smiled. If only they knew. No doubt, as Jesus and Zacchaeus walked the direction of *that* home in *that* neighborhood, some little religious stooges ran and told everything to the priests and Pharisees, who in turn would have used this as fuel to their fire to burn Jesus in effigy. After all, this was among the reasons they killed Him. He was at home with the unholy. He was full of grace, and they had no room for it. They had never experienced it or thought of themselves as in need of it. But Jesus came to call sinners, not the righteous. They brought Him such joy when they repented. They still do. Heaven throws a party every time a lost sinner is saved (Luke 15:6-7).

A few years ago, some of the members at my church raised concerns about people coming from the local rescue mission. Among the requirements in their rehab program was for people to get their spiritual life in order. They had been so hardened by life, yet they were so ready for change. One day, these members cornered me and whispered, "Pastor, we don't know if you've noticed, but we are starting to get some *icky* people in our church, and we just don't like it. We need to be very careful." *Let me take your picture. I'll show you icky* (things pastors think to themselves while trying to hold a look of sincere concern).

That conversation didn't go well. One person even said, "I am called to quarantine my family from the world." Only problem is, that's not the heart of Christ. I can't understand church people who lack compassion for the lost.

Strategy #5: Encourage Them with Assurance When They Repent

What happened next was miraculous. Zacchaeus was a dead man who came to life. The chief of sinners was remade by the Friend of Sinners. We don't know all they discussed in the back-and-forth, but

I can imagine the joy on Jesus's face when the crook said, "Behold, Lord, the half of my goods I give to the poor. And if I have defrauded anyone of anything, I restore it fourfold" (Luke 19:8).

The word "Lord" tells us who was in charge now. Jesus was. True repentance had taken place. This mobster was giving away half of his possessions to the poor. He was a changed man. The rest he would give to those whom he had made poor—those whom he had defrauded, wringing them out of their money through falsehood.

Here, Zacchaeus showed that he knew enough of the Bible to realize that stealing required making restitution, but God never commanded fourfold restoration like Zacchaeus had pledged. God only required one-fifth—that is, 20 percent. This man was so ready to make things right that he wanted to go back to everyone he had wronged and personally repay them 400 percent! That would leave him empty-handed. It didn't matter. His hands were now full of another treasure: Jesus, who is the Treasure of treasures. Zacchaeus showed evidence of true salvation.

This is critical to remember when you think about your guy friends. Repentance is necessary for salvation. It is a change of mind that results in a change of life. It's putting off old attitudes and actions and replacing them with righteous, Godward ones (Isaiah 55:6-9; Ephesians 4:20-24). It's a complete disowning of self and a life commitment to follow Christ as Lord of all (Matthew 16:24-27). The gospel is an exchange of all that I am for all that He is.

No repentance, no salvation.

It might be tempting, especially because these guys are your friends, to soften the message and make light of the command to repent. You might be inclined to hold back because you don't want to say anything that will cost you the relationship. Yet a true friend won't let his bro believe a lie, especially one that will eternally condemn him. Repentance is not something to add after salvation; it's something that happens or salvation hasn't happened:

- "Bear fruit in keeping with repentance" (Matthew 3:8).
- "Why do you call me 'Lord, Lord,' and not do what I tell you?" (Luke 6:46).
- "The times of ignorance God overlooked, but now he commands all people everywhere to repent" (Acts 17:30).

Be sure to give someone assurance of salvation only when he has genuinely repented of his sins. And once he has repented, let it flow. The joy on Jesus's face must have been matched by the relief in Zacchaeus's eyes when the Savior responded, "Today salvation has come to this house, since he also is a son of Abraham" (Luke 19:9).

What an astonishing declaration this would have been to the man who had previously denied the faith! The prodigal had come home and received full rights of sonship. In Galatians 3:7, Paul would offer the same assurance to all who believe: "Know then that it is those of faith who are the sons of Abraham."

If Jesus can save Zacchaeus and you, He can save anybody—right? Same with your lost friends. Isaiah 59:1 says, "Behold, the Lord's hand is not shortened, that it cannot save." Don't give up on those who need Christ. God has chosen to spread the news about salvation by those who have partaken of it. He goes before you and delights to use you.

Not on Your Pit Crew

The difference between Zacchaeus and the other friends in this book is this: An unbelieving guy is not on your pit crew. He is in the stands eating pretzels with mustard and drinking a bacon-infused chocolate shake. Yet he is steadily watching you during the race. Some guys in your life want to come just to see a nasty spinout, unfortunately. Other guys want to see you take a swig of milk with a wreath around your neck. Whatever your friend's reasons for watching, he may see your victories, but he doesn't participate in them. He is eyeing you through the catch-fence. Your job is to show him what Christianity looks like at every turn.

As your Zacchaeus gets to know you, invite him to take a walk down Pit Road with an all-access pit pass. Get him out of the stands and give him a taste of the action from the garage to the infield. Unlike the photo-op and autograph of a prerace cold pass, he needs to be near the live action. Let him see all, hear all, and smell all—up close, while you are in motion. Show his eyes what salvation looks like under the hood. Blow out his eardrums with the roaring engine of divine truth. Fill his nostrils with the exhaust of gospel fragrance until his eyes water. This is no time for selfies. Eternity is coming. "Whoever captures souls is wise" (Proverbs 11:30).

Important Takeaways to Remember

- Your list of friendships should include those who do not yet know the Lord.

- We must never let ourselves be so "Christian" that we lose contact with the non-Christian world.

- Reaching the lost has more to do with heart than strategy. Get Christ's heart for the lost and the strategy will follow naturally. Implement the strategy without the heart, and it will not bear lasting fruit.

- Everyone in the world is exactly where God wants them because He is orchestrating their lives to come under the hearing of the gospel. And He has put you in proximity to them for that purpose.

- Today is the day of salvation. We cannot let our hearts grow cold with the realities of eternal punishment that await those who have not yet trusted in Jesus.

- Stepping into others' lives can be messy and risky, but that cannot stop us from extending the grace that has been extended to us.

- Be sure that you don't hold back assurance from those who truly repent, but at the same time, don't give false assurance to those who do not repent.

Finding Your Zacchaeus

Earlier in this chapter, you were asked to write down the names of men in your life who need Christ. Right now would be an excellent time to fire off a text to each of the guys on your list and set up a lunch meeting or activity together. No more hesitating. Do it before you talk yourself out of it. Feed them hot wings and give them Jesus. The following practical steps will help you get started.

1. Download a Bible app on your smartphone if you haven't already and do a search for *heaven* and for *hell*. Below, write descriptions of these very real places where real people will spend a real eternity. Think of the people on your list and ask God to give you the dedication of Jonathan Edwards, who wrote at age 17, "Resolved: To endeavor to my utmost to act as I can imagine I would if I had already seen all the happiness of heaven, as well as the torments of hell."

2. Read the story of Jesus's sending of the 72 in Luke 10:1-12. Trace the strategy He laid out before His barely ready followers. Notice especially the "son of peace"—that person whose heart and sphere of influence is open for you to bring the message of Christ. Stop now and pray, asking the Lord to show you where He is already at work around you. If you have become insulated from unbelievers, consider engaging

people in places where they gather in the culture: athletic, academic, civic, political, medical, corporate, military, arts and entertainment, or media. Write down a couple of options that appeal to you, and take steps now to "be where they are."

3. Where do you get stuck most often when sharing the gospel with someone who doesn't know Jesus yet? Are you fearful you could lose the friendship? Do you feel inadequate, like you don't know enough or won't be able to answer their objections? Start simple—tell them the story of how you came to Christ. Don't worry if you don't sound polished. Just be sure that you are clear enough about *what you believed* and *what happened to you* when you became a believer. They should be able to hear enough information in your story to know what it takes to be saved. In your own words, in two or three sentences, write what a person would need to know to receive salvation in Christ.

4. Dig deeper: Purchase Greg Gilbert's helpful book: *What Is the Gospel?* or Nathan Busenitz's excellent volume *Reasons We Believe: 50 Lines of Evidence That Confirm the Christian Faith.* These books are short, bite-sized, and extremely helpful. Read them for helpful content for conversations you have with your non-Christian friends.

CHAPTER 7

You Need a Gracious Savior to Befriend You

almost died recently. Three times.

The Parker 425, hailed as The "Best in Desert Off-Road Adventure," is a race on a 425-mile dirt track in Parker, Arizona. My friend Todd, who races trick-trucks in the main event, invited me to come and speak to his pit crew before he began his six-hour high-speed adrenaline rush. Todd is a Christian and wanted to encourage his team to think past the event itself to the practical life lessons that would remain long after the race was over.

Being this was an off-road race, the pit didn't have a physical street address. Giving me directions required Todd to be physically at the pit, and to use the map on his phone to drop a pin and text it to me. Siri would do the rest. Let's just say Siri and I are done. On the morning of the race, as I rolled toward the city of Parker, I set Siri to navigate me to the pin. I soon noticed the path she guided me toward made me glad I drove my 4x4. The sand was getting deeper and the road banks were getting higher. It was the kind of terrain where I knew that if I stopped I would get stuck, so I gunned the engine. As I reacted obediently to the mechanical voice emanating from my iPhone, I saw ropes with pink ribbons and signs with arrows pointing the opposite direction—my direction. I was on the track! What I didn't know was that while my friend was preparing for the main event, several other races were happening that day. The track was live!

Just then I looked up and saw people perched on the hillside waving at me. They weren't saying, "Hello!" They were there to watch the race. I was not nearly as panicked as I should have been, but I ripped the wheel around to get off the track. About eight seconds later, embarrassment turned to horror as the lead car from the race whizzed by me going between 90-100 miles per hour on the track where I had been. Two other off-road cars followed right behind him while an orange helicopter flew about 30 feet over the lead car, keeping pace and filming. The videographer had almost filmed my death. There is no way I would have survived that collision, and neither would the race cars that would have plowed into me.

"In one mile, turn right" the GPS said. As I studied the pin I decided to venture on, but concluded that rough terrain was better. At least then I could be sure I was not on the track. I drove over desert bushes, around desert trees and cacti, and according to Siri, I was getting closer. Except in the middle of the desert, GPS doesn't work that great, because there was no signal. Thankfully, I could see the area where the pit crews were lined up way off in the distance, and worked my way closer, only to find myself surrounded by pink ribbons and arrows again. I had wandered onto the track a second time! This time people were lining the track, but they didn't notice me because they were cheering for something on the other side of the hill, which I was rapidly approaching. Whatever it was, we were coming toward each other. I did a hard 180-degree turn and sped off the track, but as I turned, the steering wheel didn't feel right. My Acura MDX was starting to act up. I was losing power and every light on the dash was lit. Turns out I had shredded my serpentine belt, but the good news was that I could see about a mile of trailers and pit crews in front of me.

Finally back on pavement, I got plenty of stares as I sputtered slowly down the pit crew lane, going the wrong direction again, where race cars were pulling off the track to get serviced. A crash would not have been as devastating if one of those cars had hit me, but as I got off pit row and rolled to a stop, I felt relief and fatigue.

"Arrived." *Thanks, Siri.* I looked up and there it was: "Milk-N-It Motorsports." My friend is a dairy-farmer. I met with the crew, gave the devotion (the topic was "Do not fear!"), cheered for my friend, and headed for home. As I drove away, I discovered that the proper entrance/exit to the race was only 500 yards from where Siri sent me in the wrong direction. As I lay on the concrete in the AutoZone parking lot changing my serpentine belt, I rehearsed the day's lessons for life, which I almost lost that day: stay on track, listen to the right voices, you can be so close yet so far, etc.

Perhaps the most long-lasting lesson of that day was the fact that I had been in serious danger and hadn't known it at first. By the time I realized I had no idea where I was going, I had shredded my vehicle, and the pit crew was nowhere to be found. The Christian life is like that. There are days coming when you could get into a dangerous situation spiritually and your pit crew won't be able to get to you. It will just be you on the track. None of your friends will be able to find or rescue you, and your efforts to rescue yourself may end up getting you into worse trouble. When that day comes, you need the most important friend in your life—Jesus Christ.

The Greatest Friend of All

In the race of life, Jesus is not just another member of the crew. He owns you, the car, the track, and the whole enterprise—your aim should be to finish well and please Him. He is Savior, Lord, and Friend. Your best Friend. While everything in this book is about the friendships that will help you strive for spiritual victory, each of those relationships is meant to point you to the greatest Friend of all, the one who "sticks closer than a brother" (Proverbs 18:24).

When you think about Jesus and His friendships, I find it fascinating that Jesus was friendly toward all, but friends with only a few. I was certain that as I searched the Scriptures to find verses relating to our friendship with Christ that there would be many. It turns out I was wrong.

Jesus speaks of friendship in passing in John 11:11, when He told His disciples that He intended to raise Lazarus from the dead: "Our friend Lazarus has fallen asleep, but I go to awaken him." In Luke 12:4, Jesus called the multitudes around him "friends" in a gesture of kindness. In parables, Jesus uses the word "friend" to describe our relationships with one other,[8] but none of them are really about us with Him. Religious hypocrites ridiculed Jesus because He had affinity for unsaved people. They gave Him the mean yet wonderful title "friend of...sinners" (Matthew 11:19). Otherwise, the closest we seem to get to the language of friendship for anyone with Jesus is in the Garden of Gethsemane with Judas Iscariot. After Judas planted the kiss of betrayal on Jesus, our Lord said to him, "Friend, do what you came to do" (Matthew 26:50). Even in that instance He used a less intimate word. Not the example I was looking for.

A Key Passage

That leaves one scripture in the entire New Testament where Jesus spoke of our friendship to Him, making it the most important and definitive teaching of Jesus on friendship anywhere in the Bible, and it is extraordinary:

> This is my commandment, that you love one another as I have loved you. Greater love has no one than this, that someone lay down his life for his friends. You are my friends if you do what I command you. No longer do I call you servants, for the servant does not know what his master is doing; but I have called you friends, for all that I have heard from my Father I have made known to you. You did not choose me, but I chose you and appointed you that you should go and bear fruit and that your fruit should abide, so that whatever you ask the Father in my name, he may give it to you. These things I command you, so that you will love one another (John 15:12-17).

These words, spoken on the eve of Jesus's crucifixion, are among His most important. They are the truths that were supposed to ring in the disciples' ears long after He was gone, and they are the principles that still define our relationship with Him now.

A Key Phrase

Here's the most important phrase in that passage: "No longer do I call you servants, for the servant does not know what his master is doing; but I have called you friends." The word Jesus used for a servant, or slave, is not an intimate term. In fact, quite the opposite.

Slaves had no real relationship with masters. They had no rights, privileges, reputation, status, or property. They were not allowed to have a will of their own. Their entire lives were tied to the master they served. And did you know that this term "slave," as used in the New Testament, defines a Christian's relationship with Christ? Throughout the New Testament, the apostles spoke of themselves and all believers using this very word, often translated "servant" or "bondservant."[9]

But notice that Jesus does something incredible. He says, "No longer do I call you servants...but I have called you friends." He tells the disciples that they have moved from slave into the realm of friendship, and not just friendship with Jesus, but irrevocable friendship. The language is in the perfect tense: "I have called you friends." *You are now and forever will be My friends, always.*

Perhaps Jesus had in mind the teaching of Exodus 21:5-6, which describes a slave who is offered release from his master but doesn't go because he has come to love his lord: "If the slave plainly says, 'I love my master, my wife, and my children; I will not go out free,' then his master shall bring him to God, and he shall bring him to the door or the doorpost. And his master shall bore his ear through with an awl, and he shall be his slave forever." Still a slave, but now a friend—a dear friend committed to a lifelong bond.

This would have been wonderful for the disciples to hear. The God-man, the Creator of the universe, Messiah, Savior of the world, was extending eternal friendship to them, and nothing could take it away. But then, as if to burst their balloon, in John 16:7, Jesus shocked them with the news that He was going to leave: "Nevertheless, I tell you the truth: it is to your advantage that I go away" (insert sound of brakes screeching).

If I had been in the room, I would have said, "What do You

mean it's to their advantage? Have You seen what these guys are like when You aren't with them? You can't leave! Everything falls apart when You are more than fifty feet away." And yet Jesus continued to repeat that leaving was a good thing (14:2-3, 18-19, 28-29; 16:28). Why was it good? Look at the rest of John 16:7: "If I do not go away, the Helper will not come to you. But if I go, I will send him to you."

A Key Transition

Stunning! It was better for Jesus to leave and for the Holy Spirit to come than for Jesus to have stayed with them. How? Jesus's unexpected answer comes in John 14:17: "…the Spirit of truth, whom the world cannot receive, because it neither sees him nor knows him. You know him, for he dwells with you and will be in you."

Jesus had been *with* them, but His Spirit would dwell *in* them, and that is infinitely better. By His Spirit, He would remain with them, though He Himself was physically going to the right hand of the Father in heaven. During His ministry, Jesus taught, guided, motivated, lead, reproved, empowered, and comforted them, but at the coming of the Holy Spirit, all of those personal helps would move from external to internal. Astonishingly, Jesus *with* them was nothing compared to Jesus *in* them, by His Spirit.

This helps us understand our relationship with Jesus better. When Jesus attaches the reality of His friendship with us, to His Spirit in us, it becomes clear that the work of the Holy Spirit is primarily to mediate our friendship with Christ from heaven, until we see Christ face to face.

Have you ever thought about the apostles and their privileged access to Christ, and wished you'd had that same experience? To hear Him teach the Scriptures, to watch Him calm a storm or walk on water, to see Him ruin funerals by raising the dead, to feel the burn after He bested the Pharisees, to watch demons cower before Him, or to see lepers' faces reappear at His touch—it seems that would have made it a lot easier to have a friendship with Christ. They knew what Jesus looked like, how His voice sounded, whether He snored and told jokes. They would've certainly felt like insiders when they saw God incarnate brush His teeth. Wouldn't you have enjoyed that kind of backstage pass access? Of course you would.

Now, be honest—have you ever thought to yourself, *That would have been amazing! But me, all I have is the Holy Spirit?* I've thought that before, mistakenly.

According to Jesus, having the Holy Spirit is better—Jesus *in* us is better than Jesus *with* us. We diminish our relationship with Christ when we fail to see the advantage of the indwelling Holy Spirit over the physical presence of Jesus with us at all times. It's hard to believe, but that's what Jesus said. From Pentecost onward, all who believed would experience something far greater in their friendship with Christ than they ever could have had during the ministry of Christ on earth—the indwelling Holy Spirit. This is also the truest and purest understanding of the ministry of the Holy Spirit—to point us to Christ. For example, the Holy Spirit

- illuminates the Scriptures so that we might welcome the truth about Christ.
- convicts us of sin so that we might be restored to fellowship with Christ.
- empowers us with spiritual gifts so that we might joyfully serve Christ.
- emboldens us to stand up against persecution for the sake of Christ.
- fills us with truth to clearly proclaim the gospel of Christ.

- works in us that we might bear fruit for the glory of Christ.

- secures our salvation for the day when we will be presented to Christ.

What Friendship with Jesus Looks Like

The only question that remains is this: What does a friendship with Christ look like now, while He is in heaven? Knowing this will help us press into Him until the day we see him face to face. Thankfully, Jesus invites us to enjoy His friendship in five ways.

Invitation #1: Savor His Love

When Jesus announced that the disciples were His friends, He declared His love for them with these familiar, life-changing words, "Greater love has no one than this, that someone lay down his life for his friends. You are my friends" (John 15:13-14). Love displayed in sacrifice is the highest virtue in the commitment of a friendship. And that is exactly what Jesus would do for them, and us, just a few hours after these words were spoken.

He would go to the cross and be slain. He would give His righteous life as an offering, in our place. He would willingly subject Himself to beatings, and allow His beard to be ripped out and spit to drip from His face. He voluntarily came under the pressure of bearing God's fierce wrath, the thought of which made blood leak out of His pores. His love didn't let Him retaliate to the mocking, taunting, and hate. He was beaten to a pulp, stripped naked, nailed to a tree, suspended in the air, suffocated to death, stabbed in the heart, and laid in a tomb—all for love, all for us. That's His contribution to our friendship, a love measured by the depth of sacrifice.

That sacrifice opened access for us to have salvation, full and free.

It includes the forgiveness of our sins, a new heart, strength against temptation, victory over Satan, and the hope of future glory. Our past is cleared, our future is secured, and our present is empowered. He's taken care of everything. Nothing stands in the way of the relationship He made us and saved us to experience. Our friendship with Christ was purchased by Him with His great love. Now, savor that.

As dinner continued that night, the Savior spoke about our friendship with Him as a reciprocal exchange of love—His ongoing love for us and our grateful response of love for Him.

- "If you love me, you will keep my commandments" (John 14:15).
- "Whoever has my commandments and keeps them, he it is who loves me. And he who loves me will be loved by my Father, and I will love him and manifest myself to him" (John 14:21).
- "If anyone loves me, he will keep my word, and my Father will love him, and we will come to him and make our home with him" (John 14:23).
- "As the Father has loved me, so have I loved you. Abide in my love. If you keep my commandments, you will abide in my love, just as I have kept my Father's commandments and abide in his love" (John 15:9-10).
- "The Father himself loves you, because you have loved me and have believed that I came from God" (John 16:27).

Jesus would affirm the depth of God's love for us in John 17:23 when He expressed to His Father how He "loved them even as you loved me." Jesus loves us to the depth that He would give His life for us, and the Father loves us as much as He loves Jesus. The Holy

Spirit will keep us in that love, give us the ability to reciprocate it, and give it to others (15:12,17; see also Romans 5:5).

Do you want a closer friendship with Jesus? Meditate on His sacrifice at the cross until you find yourself resolved with Isaac Watts to respond, "Were the whole realm of nature mine, that were a present far too small; love so amazing, so divine, demands my soul, my life, my all."[10] Then give all that you are and all that you have to Him in return.

If this were the beginning and end of our friendship with Christ, it would be more than enough for all eternity, but there's more.

Invitation #2: Experience His Life

Immediately after Jesus declared we are His friends, He said, "You did not choose me, but I chose you and appointed you that you should go and bear fruit and that your fruit should abide" (John 15:16). In one of the clearest statements of the sovereign grace of salvation, Jesus informed them that (1) He initiated this friendship by a decision of His own will, uninfluenced; and (2) He did it with the goal in mind that we would "bear fruit" that would remain.

In the Bible, "fruit" is always a metaphor for good works. The most familiar passage related to bearing fruit is Galatians 5:22-23: "The fruit of the Spirit is love, joy, peace, patience, kindness, goodness, faithfulness, gentleness, self-control" (notice the connection to the Holy Spirit).

But when Jesus mentioned fruit in connection to our friendship with Him, it was a topic He was already discussing. Just a few verses earlier, He had said:

> I am the true vine, and my Father is the vinedresser. Every branch in me that does not bear fruit he takes away, and every branch that does bear fruit he prunes, that it may

bear more fruit. Already you are clean because of the word that I have spoken to you. Abide in me, and I in you. As the branch cannot bear fruit by itself, unless it abides in the vine, neither can you, unless you abide in me. I am the vine; you are the branches. Whoever abides in me and I in him, he it is that bears much fruit, for apart from me you can do nothing... By this my Father is glorified, that you bear much fruit and so prove to be my disciples (John 15:1-5, 8).

A true Christian, by definition, is a fruit-bearer. His good works not only glorify God, they furnish proof that he is a genuine believer. But don't miss the main point: We bear fruit only because we draw our life from Jesus. In the same way that a vine sends life-giving sap from the root of the plant to produce the fruit of the plant, our life comes from His life. And all the while, the Father is actively at work in us, pruning us by cutting away all the sucker branches so they can't drain away our spiritual vitality, causing us to "bear more fruit."

My mentor, Jay Letey, once asked me a question I've never forgotten. He said, "When Christ came to live in you, what did He come to do?" As I raced mentally for the exegetically and theologically correct answer, he quipped, "You're thinking too hard. When Christ came to live in you, what did He come to do?" Then after a few more moments of pause, he relieved my burden and said, "The answer is in the question: 'When Christ came to live in you, what did He come to do?' He came to live in you!" Jay showed me how easy it is for me to make Christianity hard. It doesn't need to be. At its core, Christianity is about Christ's life in us, by His Spirit, in an eternal, spiritual friendship. Once we get that right, we can experience His life in a variety of ways. Here are a few that Jesus mentioned to His disciples:

His Presence with You

In John 14:17, speaking of the Holy Spirit, Jesus said, "You know him, for he dwells with you and will be in you." Don't forget, the Holy Spirit is the Spirit of Christ. He is called the "Spirit of Jesus" (Acts 16:7), the "Spirit of Christ" (Romans 8:9), and the "Spirit of his Son" (Galatians 4:6). The Holy Spirit is not another God. He is one and the same in essence and nature as the Father and Son, the third person of the Trinity. If you have Him, you have Jesus. Not *with* you, but *in* you. Jesus reminded His disciples at the Great Commission, "I am with you always, even to the end of the age" (Matthew 28:20). How is that possible when He's at the right hand of the Father? The answer is through His Spirit.

His Power Through You

In this same conversation, Jesus said, "Truly, truly, I say to you, whoever believes in me will also do the works that I do; and greater works than these will he do, because I am going to the Father" (John 14:12). We will do greater works than Jesus? That's what He said. Obviously not greater than the atonement itself, for no one can outdo the substitutionary sacrifice of Christ. These are works "greater" in quantity, not quality. As the incarnate Son, He was just one man who could be in only one place at one time on earth. From heaven, He can do infinitely more as He lives His life through us, by His Spirit.

His Pleasure Within You

Twice at that dinner, Jesus offered Christians a life filled with His joy: "These things I have spoken to you, that my joy may be in you, and that your joy may be full" (John 15:11), and "Until now you have asked nothing in my name. Ask, and you will receive, that your joy may be full" (16:24). Full and overflowing joy. Ultimate, comprehensive satisfaction in a Savior who loves us, whose leaving would mean even greater joy through the Spirit.

His Protection over You

Experiencing the joy of Christ would be especially hard to fake in light of Jesus's warning against the dangers that would come against us as His followers, from within and without. Satan and his temptations, the world and its hostility, and our hearts with their propensity to wander would all try to pull us away from Christ. The disciples would have been especially tempted to fear the lack of Jesus's physical presence to protect them. But His departure meant the sending of the all-sufficient Spirit, who would ensure their security. Jesus comforted them with these words: "I have said all these things to you to keep you from falling away" (John 16:1). And He finished His entire discourse with the promise, "I have said these things to you, that in me you may have peace. In the world you will have tribulation. Take heart; I have overcome the world" (verse 33). He would guard us by His Spirit.

His Peace in You

Peace is the internal confidence that all is well because God is in control. No need to fret or fear. We can stand in the center of swirling chaos and be unruffled because of an internal calm provided by Jesus through His Spirit. "Peace I leave with you; my peace I give to you. Not as the world gives do I give to you. Let not your hearts be troubled, neither let them be afraid" (John 14:27). "The fruit of the Spirit is…peace" (Galatians 5:22).

His presence with us, His power through us, His pleasure within us, His protection over us, and His peace in us—can you think of

His presence with us,

His power through us,

His pleasure within us,

His protection over us,

and His peace in us—

can you think of anything

else we would want or need

that we don't already have

through Christ via His Spirit?

We lack nothing.

anything else we would want or need that we don't already have through Christ via His Spirit? We lack nothing. "Yet a little while and the world will see me no more, but you will see me. Because I live, you also will live" (John 14:19).

Invitation #3: Know His Truth

Following His declaration that forever we will be His friends, Jesus described the nuance of our friendship in terms of close, first-hand, intimate knowledge. He said, "No longer do I call you servants, for the servant does not know what his master is doing; but I have called you friends, *for all that I have heard from my Father I have made known to you*" (John 15:15, emphasis added). According to Jesus, friendship equals disclosure; intimacy equals revelation. That's what a friend does. He gives you close, personal information. He tells you things he doesn't tell others. As our Friend, Jesus said that He would tell us everything we need to know about Him and His will, which He also ties back to the Holy Spirit:

- "These things I have spoken to you while I am still with you. But the Helper, the Holy Spirit, whom the Father will send in my name, he will teach you all things and bring to your remembrance all that I have said to you" (John 14:25-26).

- "But when the Helper comes, whom I will send to you from the Father, the Spirit of truth, who proceeds from the Father, he will bear witness about me" (John 15:26).

- "I still have many things to say to you, but you cannot bear them now. When the Spirit of truth comes, he will guide you into all the truth, for he will not speak on his own authority, but whatever he hears he will speak, and he will declare to you the things that are to come. He will glorify me, for he will take what is mine and declare it to you. All that the Father has is mine; therefore I said that he will take what is mine and declare it to you" (John 16:12-15).

In a world without clarity, Jesus promised that we can cultivate our friendship with Him without confusion. The Holy Spirit would see to it. We will always have the truth because the resident Truth-teacher always dwells in us. To be precise, Jesus was not referring to an individual believer's unique special revelation, but rather the inspired revelation of Scripture. He was talking about the New Testament. Some of the men in that very room would write it down, guided by the Holy Spirit. The Spirit of Jesus would remind them exactly of what He did and said, as well as reveal, clarify, explain, and apply more truth about the person, work, and coming of Christ.

This gift of inspiration would produce a body of doctrine that would be passed down to all generations so that anyone could have access to Christ. But the fact that Jesus tied the Scriptures to us in terms of friendship means the Bible is not an abstract book with categories of doctrine disconnected from our life. Everything in it is meant to help us grow in our friendship with Christ. We don't study it so that we can spout out big words like *prolegomena*, *hamartiaology*, *soteriology*, *pneumatology*, and *eschatology*. It's not so that we can win arguments in theological debates, or impress people as if godliness was defined only by knowledge (1 Corinthians 8:1). The truth of Christ, however, given to us by the Spirit of Christ, is meant to drive us closer to the person of Christ.

So dig into your Bible and ransack its truths to find Jesus. Go under and hold your breath as long as you can, and come up only to get more air so that you can go back under. Take Bible classes, listen to good sermons, read good Christian books that explain the Bible and draw attention to Jesus. Go as deep as you can. Then take everything you learn, and don't rest until it's made you closer to Christ. He has been a good Friend to reveal the truth; be a good friend in return and love the truth (2 Thessalonians 2:10).

Invitation #4: Obey His Authority

All this talk about our friendship with Christ, properly understood, shouldn't make you feel like you have to approach Jesus with sappy sentimentalism. Quite the opposite. It is the height of biblical masculinity to lean in on Jesus. And while we no longer relate to Him as distant slaves, but as dear friends, that doesn't minimize His authority in our lives. He is still our Lord. Jesus makes that clear: "You are my friends if you do what I command you" (John 15:14). He made sure we still understand the responsibility of obedience.

- "If you keep my commandments, you will abide in my love, just as I have kept my Father's commandments and abide in his love" (John 15:10).
- "This is my commandment, that you love one another as I have loved you" (John 15:12).
- "These things I command you, so that you will love one another" (John 15:17).

Did you also notice how Jesus describes our obedience as commands motivated by His love for us, and our love for Him (see also John 14:14,23)? Everything is tied to friendship, as it should be. This is a far greater motive for obedience than mere slavery. We don't have to obey out of compulsion or fear, but rather, we can obey out of love and joy, for His pleasure.

Invitation #5: Exalt His Glory

Jesus rounds out His teaching about friendship with an invitation. He tells us to keep seeking whatever we might need from Him until the day we see Him face-to-face. He invites us to pray with the expectation that "whatever you ask the Father in my name, he may give it to you" (John 15:16). To be clear, this is an invitation to ask for the things that a cross-centered, joy-filled, truth-loving, fruit-bearing friend of Christ would want. It's not a blank check that lets you use "in Jesus's name" as if it was a magical incantation to gratify your flesh. Prayers offered in Jesus's name are supposed to be consistent with Jesus's will and character. They are requests for what brings Him glory. If what you ask for will bring glory to Him, He will say, "Yes!" We know that's what He means because one chapter earlier, He said, "Whatever you ask in my name, this I will do, that the Father may be glorified in the Son" (John 14:13).

This also is the work of the Holy Spirit, according to Jesus. He said, "When the Spirit of truth comes, he will guide you into all the truth, for he will not speak on his own authority, but whatever he hears he will speak, and he will declare to you the things that are to come. *He will glorify me*" (John 16:13-14, emphasis added). Everything the Holy Spirit does on our behalf to strengthen our friendship with Christ is done so that Christ will be exalted. The Spirit's goal is to help you realize how truly great Christ is so that you will go after Him as hard as you can, and let go of the banal trivialities of this world that masquerade as lasting joy but only offer passing pleasure.

The Spirit convinces you that Christ is the Treasure hidden in the field—a treasure so great that it's worth selling the whole field to have Him because of the sheer pleasure He brings (Matthew 13:44). He compels you to say with the apostle Paul:

Whatever gain I had, I counted as loss for the sake of Christ. Indeed, I count everything as loss because of the surpassing worth of knowing Christ Jesus my Lord. For his sake I have suffered the loss of all things and count them as rubbish, in order that I may gain Christ and be found in him, not having a righteousness of my own that comes from the law, but that which comes through faith in Christ, the righteousness from God that depends on faith—that I may know him (Philippians 3:7-10).

The Holy Spirit gives your life perspective because He teaches you to say, "For to me to live is Christ, and to die is gain" (Philippians 1:21). And as you march toward that final day when you will see Jesus in person and your soul will know the thrill for which it was made, the Holy Spirit will give you to Christ, for whom He has sealed you (Ephesians 1:13-14).

After the Checkered Flag

When at last you have crossed the finish line under the checkered flag and your race is over, Christ Himself will welcome you, perfect you, and reward you. All you have given up will be repaid. All your past sufferings will be replaced by comfort. All you have done for Him will be celebrated. All you have wasted will be forgotten.

And on that day, you will realize that Jesus Christ was truly your best friend. You will see that He was the one who provided each of the men in your pit crew, and that it was He who worked through them as you made your way to victory. While He had supplied you with a Paul to be your crew chief, He was your actual source of wisdom. Although He had given you a Barnabas for a tire-changer, He was the one who held you on the track. Though He had provided a Jonathan to be there as your fuel man, He was the one who replenished you as your best Friend. When He sent a Nathan to you with a fire extinguisher, Jesus Himself was your chastisement and your peace. Though your own Timothy offered the support of a jack-man, the undergirding you received and the example you set all came from Him. And for the entire race from start to finish—including your salvation, your hope, your victory—Jesus was alongside you as the crew chief.

As you continue racing on the track, the Spirit of God within you is urging you to push the gas pedal harder, to wipe away the dust from your eyes so you can see clearer, and to go as strong as you can until you cross the finish line. Then after you've taken your victory lap and you hear the roar from the cloud of witnesses, you will scarcely be able to contain yourself as Jesus calls you up to the platform to join Him in the winner's circle, where He will award you the prize for having finished well. Yours will be the victory, and His will be the glory.

The only question left is this: Is that how you want to finish in life? Then after you finish reading this book, put it down and go find your crew. Ask God to bring the right people into your life. Utilize their strengths and benefit from what they have to offer you.

And when it's all over, bring them with you to Victory Lane.

Important Takeaways to Remember

- There's a day coming when you end up in dangerous situations spiritually and your pit crew won't be able to get to you. When that day comes, you need the most important friend in your life—Jesus Christ.

- Jesus is not on your pit crew; He is the owner. He owns you, the car, the track, and the whole enterprise. Your aim should be to please Him and finish well.

- Each of the relationships mentioned in this book is meant to point you to the greatest Friend of all, Jesus.

- Jesus said it was better for Him to leave and for the Holy Spirit to come than for Him to have stayed with us. That's because Jesus *in* us, by His Spirit, is better than Jesus *with* us.

- The primary work of the Holy Spirit is to mediate our friendship with Christ from heaven until we see Jesus face to face.

- Jesus loves us to the depth that He would give His life for us, and the Father loves us as much as He loves Jesus.

- The fact that Jesus ties the giving of Scripture to us in terms of friendship means the Bible is not an abstract book with categories of doctrine disconnected from our life. Everything in it is meant to help us grow in our friendship with Christ.

- Jesus's Spirit ensures that we will always have Jesus's presence with us, His power through us, His pleasure within us, His protection over us, and His peace in us. There is nothing else we would want or need that we don't already have through Christ via His Spirit! We lack nothing.

- Jesus has provided you with each of the men in your pit crew, and it is He who works through them to bring about your victory. He is your crew chief—the one who equips the tire changer, fuel man, fire extinguisher person, and jack-man to carry out their roles.

- Though Jesus gives us the victory, the glory is His alone.

Finding Your Savior

If you don't know Christ as your personal Lord and Savior, He invites you to enter into a friendship with Him at this moment. But before you can do that, you need to talk to Him about sin. He made you, but you've rebelled against Him. He loves you, but your heart is dark and can't love Him back. He died and rose again for you, but you have to believe in Him. He stands ready to forgive you, but you must ask Him. You are a criminal standing before the Judge of the Universe, and He is holding the pardon in His hand. Right now you can go free, be forgiven, transformed from within, and given the promise of eternal life. The Judge will become your Friend.

1. If you want to enter into an eternal relationship with Jesus Christ as Savior and Lord, review the following scriptures and let them guide you as you cry out to Him to give you what they promise: Romans 5:8-10; 10:9-10; 1 Peter 3:18; Luke 18:9-14.

2. Stir your heart in the love that made Christ lay down His life for us. I recommend starting a Bible reading plan just through the New Testament, using a highlighter, in which you mark every verse that mentions Jesus's death or His love. Once you have gone from Matthew to Revelation, go back and read

those highlighted verses again. Do this at regular intervals in the months and years ahead.

3. As you ponder the presence, power, pleasure, protection, and peace of Christ available to you, which one would you say you need most in your life right now? Jesus promised that His Spirit would give you all of these in full to hold you until you see Him. How does what you learned in this chapter compel you to respond Christ as your Friend?

4. Can you point to any area of your life where your spiritual pit crew is ignorant of a problem under the hood that needs immediate attention? They don't know about it yet, but you do, and Jesus does. Would you go to Jesus with it right now and confess it? Would you forsake it and invite the men in

your life to carry your burden to Jesus with you? Don't get out on the track like I did without any help and face your problem alone. Seeking the help of your pit crew—and Jesus—can help you to experience victory.

CHAPTER 8

Anyone Can Finish Well

Race-car driving is among one of the more dangerous sports in the world. In the NASCAR series, for a period of three to four hours, 43 cars, each weighing 3,300 pounds, thunder around the track at speeds of 150-200 miles per hour. They're all competing for first place. Every guy who lines up revving his engine while waiting for the green envisions himself swigging a bottle of milk at the end of the day. However, every driver knows that even the most experienced racers are vulnerable to tragedy. At some point in the race, every competitor will experience problems, and if they are not addressed, they could not only jeopardize the victory, but take a life.

On February 18, 2001, tragedy struck race-car legend Dale Earnhardt on the last turn of his last lap in the Daytona 500. As he was approaching the finish line, Dale's famous No. 3 car was in third place when it came into light contact with the car driven by Sterling Marlin. The little bump sent Earnhardt into car No. 36 (Ken Schrader) and the retaining wall at a 55-degree angle. The entangled pair slowly slid off the asphalt to a stop in the infield grass as the finisher, Michael Waltrip, started his victory lap. Emergency responders descended on Earnhardt's car, but it took only seconds for concern to turn into panic. The greatest race-car driver in modern history was in full cardiac arrest. As crews raced against the clock to tear the roof off the Goodwrench car, the first responders discovered what no one in the racing world was prepared to hear: The 49-year-old NASCAR legend, who had won 76 Winston Cup races, had died almost instantly of blunt force trauma to the head.

If you watch the video, the crash was fairly unspectacular, especially when you compare his wreck with some of the more severe crashes in history. In a sport where cars have literally lifted off the ground, flipped end over end, caught on fire, and been pummeled by other cars going speeds in excess of 150 miles per hour, we have become accustomed to watching the driver climb out of the vehicle with only minor bumps and scrapes. But there are times when a racer isn't so fortunate.

The lessons for our Christian lives are strikingly parallel: You could be the greatest driver in history, but you are not immune to a catastrophe. You could have several victories under your belt and a trophy case that reminds you that you are a champion, but that is no guarantee of future victory. Even if you start on the inside front row in the pole position, anything can go wrong. It could come all the way down to the last turn of your last lap, and all it takes is a little bump, and you are done.

How You Finish Is Up to You

This book is about you finishing well in the race of life with the help of those who are committed to your personal spiritual victory.

Like high-performance race cars, we are all driven by a God-given power train that surges us forward, but finishing well is not a given. If you are a Christian, you *will* finish. But *how* you finish is up to you.

You may have come to the end of this book wondering if anyone can really finish well. Maybe you are a new believer and you feel like you are just getting started with so little time left—everyone else seems 100 laps ahead, and there is just no way to catch them. Maybe you have seen so many examples of failure that you wonder whether finishing well is even possible. Or maybe you yourself have crashed and burned, with no idea how to begin again. You could be climbing out of the rubble, not even sure the extent of your injuries. If so, this book's final chapter is your new starting line.

In this chapter, I want us to view the race from the perspective of a man who had experienced one of the worst crashes in biblical history and lived to tell about it. He lost control, flipped over, and flamed out, but he also got back in his car and finished strong. He didn't walk away unscathed, but he did emerge as the kind of man we all want to be. His name is Simon Peter, and his 11-car pileup began during his last conversation with Jesus before the cross:

> "Simon, Simon, behold, Satan demanded to have you, that he might sift you like wheat, but I have prayed for you that your faith may not fail. And when you have turned again, strengthen your brothers." Peter said to him, "Lord, I am ready to go with you both to prison and to death." Jesus said, "I tell you, Peter, the rooster will not crow this day, until you deny three times that you know me" (Luke 22:31-34).

This familiar story gives us tremendous insight into how we spin out in the Christian race, as well as how to avoid doing that. The metaphor of choice that Jesus used to communicate the danger to Peter is the word "sift." The Greek word translated "sift" is an agricultural term that describes the way farmers harvested wheat. When the crop was ripe for picking, the wheat was cut down and placed in a pile on the threshing floor. An ox was yoked to a large rolling pin, which was pulled back and forth over the grain, crushing the outer shell that housed the cereal within. After the husks were broken repeatedly, the farmer lifted up the pile with a pitchfork and threw it into the wind. The broken husks and wheat stalks separated from the grain in the air, and the wheat itself, being heavier than the chaff, fell back to the ground. After several rounds of crushing, stabbing, flinging, blowing, and settling, the harvester gathered his grain and stored it in his barn.

In the analogy, sifting is a severe testing—the total breaking down of a person that devastates him to the very core of his being. As a result, the one being sifted gets to see the truth about what he really is on the inside. The exterior is shattered, the facade is taken off, and all pretense is stripped away. The only thing left is the nub of that person, his true self.

Don't think of sifting as your average ordinary trial; it is a violent ordeal accompanied by pain, anxiety, and misfortune. Unlike the trial of having to wait in line at Disneyland and enjoy "The Happiest Place on Earth" at your preferred pace, sifting is what happens when you find your wife in the arms of another man; when an active shooter targets your daughter's classroom; or when the doctor says the chemo treatments won't work or the surgery is not survivable. An outdated computer, a delayed payday, and a broken wheel on a suitcase can each be a bummer, but they are nothing like the difficulty Peter was about to face. No one is ever the same after a sifting.

How to Avoid a Spinout

Peter was one of Jesus's 12 apostles, called out and raised up to represent the Savior wherever he went. He was a leader. But you might say Peter had a "need for speed." His hard-wiring inclined him to learn by deciding and doing. He took action and got results. He was a black/white, on/off, yes/no, always/never kind of man. Often wrong but never in doubt, Peter was a confident, bold risk-taker. He was the kind of alpha male whom everyone expected to win his race by several car lengths—so did he, for that matter. As a pattern, Peter had the tendency to muscle forward toward his own goal, at his own pace, and in his own power.

On the memorable evening before Jesus's crucifixion, Peter made the most common mistake in race-car driving: overdriving the car past its own capacity and design. When that happened, he modeled what not to do and taught us this critical life principle: The crashes and burns in our lives can serve the greater purpose of teaching us to finish well, if we will take the lessons we learn to heart. You may not be able to avoid a sifting, but you can avoid a spinout. Here's how:

Pay Attention to the Colored Flags

Everyone knows about the checkered flag that waves proudly over the finish line on the final lap, but there are several other flags used in auto racing, each with its own purpose. Green signals the start of the race, but it is also used later if the race has had to stop for any reason, letting the drivers know it is time to begin again. Throughout His ministry, Jesus waved this flag at Peter. For three years, Peter had been living life "in the fast lane" with Jesus and was virtually unbeatable. But on this fateful night, Jesus pulled out the yellow flag, signaling caution. Danger was ahead.

The yellow flag is a warning, indicating a hazard (usually on the track surface). When this flag is raised, drivers are required to slow down. Typically when this color comes out, the pace car enters the track and leads everyone forward at a safe, reduced speed. Sifting was coming—Peter needed to slow down, let Jesus lead, and carefully follow His speed, but Peter hadn't been paying attention. Earlier in Luke 22:24, right before Jesus waved the caution flag, Peter and the other disciples had been arguing about their favorite topic: which of them was the greatest. To bring Peter back to reality, Jesus flashed a burst of yellow in front of his eyes by calling him by his pre-salvation name, "Simon," and repeated it again for emphasis.

In Matthew 16:18, Jesus changed Simon's name to Peter after he confessed that Jesus was "the Christ, the Son of the living God" (Matthew 16:16). Jesus punctuated the moment by giving him a name which means "rocky." Peter himself was not the rock upon which Christ would build His church—that's a slightly different Greek word. Rather, the term Jesus used for Peter is more like "little pebble." And whenever Jesus called Peter by his old name, it really got his attention because it was the signal that he was acting like his old self, the guy Jesus knew before salvation. The name *Simon* would have boxed his ears and left them ringing, which was exactly what Peter needed.

The only flag Peter was interested in was black and white, yet throughout the night, Jesus's yellow flag would be replaced with a yellow-and-red striped flag: the track is slippery ahead. Later in the Garden of Gethsemane, Jesus pulled out the red flag: "Peter! Stop!" As Peter ran away while the Roman soldiers were arresting Jesus, Peter's conscience flew the black flag with the orange dot: mechanical failure, return to the pit. Finally, in the courtyard of Caiaphas's house in front of a fire, a slave girl waved the black flag that sent a message to Simon Peter that he never thought he would receive: disqualified.

Most of the time when a good guy goes down, it is not because he didn't receive a clear warning; it is because he sped past the warning that was put there to keep him safe. He thought, like we sometimes do, *I can handle it* and *It won't happen to me.* Wisdom says the opposite: "The prudent sees danger and hides himself, but the simple go on and suffer for it" (Proverbs 22:3). Do you want to avoid a spinout? Follow the flags, whether they are from God Himself, the promptings of your own conscience, or even your detractors.

Beware of the Dangers on the Road

Jesus's warning to Peter included another specific detail about a very serious danger on the road: "Behold, Satan demanded to have you, that he might sift you like wheat, but I have prayed for you" (Luke 22:31-32). The danger is the devil. Satan had asked for Peter by name. He wanted to know what this disciple was really made of. He wanted to get on the road with Peter and find out what kind of driver he was. Peter had boasted greatly of his many victories, but now it was going to be one on one.

Now, if I am Peter, my first response to Jesus is: "Well, You told him no, right? I mean, how about that hedge of protection, accompanied by some razor wire, cinder blocks, and Doberman Pinschers?" But Jesus would not spare Peter from sifting, nor will He spare us. God must tear us down so that He can build us up His way. My second response to Jesus is equally superficial and self-interested as the first: *You prayed for me? That's it? Really?* But in the sifting, Peter would learn something profound about the sufficiency of Christ and where the real power for his life came from.

Peter would be repeatedly crushed, flung helplessly into the air, dropped down to the ground, and then taken away, *by Satan himself*. And Jesus was going to let it happen. I find it comforting to know that Satan has to ask permission before he can touch us—nothing happens to us except that which first passes through the filter of God's perfect will. God is big enough to use whatever hell can unleash to make us what He wants us to be. We must not forget, however, that the devil remains the most dangerous being in the universe, and he should not be taken lightly.

The phrase "Satan has demanded to have you" is military language. It describes the way a foreign army demands the return of a soldier who is being held across enemy lines. But Satan's demand was not like that used in negotiations for a POW who should be given his freedom; it was the angry ultimatum given for one who has defected and gone AWOL, who must be returned so that he can be punished. The latter was how Satan wanted to unleash on Peter, just like he did some 2,000 years earlier with Job.

Astonishingly, Peter was not afraid. Having been kept safe in Jesus's witness protection program for the past three years and having even been quite successful at thwarting the advance of the kingdom of darkness, no doubt Peter felt ready for this next test. After all, he and the other disciples were so effective when they preached, healed, and cast out demons that Jesus said (in reference to the invisible, heavenly realm) He watched "Satan fall like lightning from heaven" (Luke 10:18). Peter felt prepared: *Bring it on!* But he had underestimated his enemy, and he had overestimated himself.

Peter's overconfidence was evident in his reply to Jesus: "Lord, I am ready to go" (Luke 22:33). In the original Greek text, this phrase also came from military language, intended to match Jesus's warning. It means to be armed and ready for battle. *Satan wants to go?*

Let's go! Peter thought he was ready. He had no idea, until he got into the boxing ring with the devil, how short his arms were. His few, controlled skirmishes with darkness were no guarantee of present strength or future success. The same is true in racing and in life: Having a high-performance race car is not enough.

A race-car driver and his pit crew are careful to run all the diagnostics before a race, to make sure the car is in top performing condition. Every detail is checked and double-checked. The driver can anticipate how his car will perform with pinpoint accuracy, but once the contest begins, there are a thousand obstacles in his way, each potentially race- or career-ending. There are so many unknowns, as Peter would soon learn.

If you look more closely at Peter's answer to Jesus, you will also see his shortsightedness and pride. He not only trusted in his past victories, but he had failed to prepare for a very different danger than any he had faced before. Peter said, "Lord, I am ready to go with you both to prison and to death" (Luke 22:33). First, Peter thought he was going to be sifted while still safe in the presence of Jesus: "I am ready to go *with you*" (emphasis added). But Jesus would not be going with him. Peter would face this trial alone. Jesus's prayers would hold Peter, but the Sustainer would be taken from him.

Recall that Peter's track record was such that anytime he was remotely distant from Christ, he fell apart. Now he was about to be totally separated from Christ and in the presence of Satan. Second, Peter thought he would face outward persecution, not inward temptation: "Lord, I am ready to go with you... *to death*" (emphasis added). He was under the impression that the worst Satan could throw at him was jail time or martyrdom, both of which Peter saw himself gloriously enduring *with Jesus*. But what he was about to face would take place apart from Jesus, and it would not be external. Sifting happens on the inside, and in this case, it would reveal that there was still too much Simon in Peter.

Heed the Warnings Inside the Car

Every racer will tell you that beyond the technical and physical aspects of the racing event, the most important preparation for the big day is mental and emotional—exactly where Peter remained unprotected. The ability to sustain this kind of fortitude for 200 laps isn't easy. The driver has to balance pushing his car to the limit of its capability without pushing too hard. He has to pay attention to things like oil pressure and water temperature. To help him, the stock car is equipped with a customized dashboard and instruments to alert him to a problem under the hood. Warning lights on the dash are like flags *inside* the car. They tell him he had better pit soon or something bad will happen. Impetuous drivers might be tempted to disregard the warnings and chance it rather than lose their lead, but that never works.

With regard to my own car, if the "Check Engine" light comes on, I know I have about two days to get the engine fixed, if not less. The first time I see the bright orange light it surprises me, but with the busyness of life, I sometimes think *I will address that tomorrow.* When tomorrow comes, I see the light again, and with less urgency I think, *You know, I wonder what that is? There does not seem to be any obvious problem with the vehicle that I can hear. I will have to get that looked at.* By day three, the light that tells me something is wrong with the most important part of my car has faded in with the other colors. If I ever happen to notice it again, my mind easily dismisses the warning: *Well, I guess it was nothing. I have driven it this far. Must*

*be a computer malfunction. The next time I get the car serviced, I will
ask them to turn off that light.*

The only thing more stupid than the neglect of a car's internal
workings is the neglect of our personal internal workings. These
problems don't just go away or fix themselves. They wear away at us
until that part of us stops working correctly, which then causes other
parts to stop working as well. Big problems in life are usually little
problems that didn't get addressed when they were little. It takes
mental discipline and emotional composure to heed the lights on
the dashboard.

However, as sensitive as the instrument panel is, there are no
lights to alert the driver to what's happening inside his body. Racing
can take a serious toll there too. Beyond what's happened under the
hood, sometimes the biggest danger on the road is inside the driver
himself. If he doesn't address the issues inside the car, he is in trouble, but if he does not correct the problems within himself, he will
experience a danger that no one can detect until it's too late.

During a race, there are several things that happen to a driver's
body that are masked by his adrenaline. For example, his body temperature is affected by the insulation of his suit, the heat of the day,
and the sun as it beats down on the asphalt. Dehydration is another
danger—we don't know how bad it is until the effects have over-
taken us. Most men can muscle through the dry mouth and slight
headache, but when rapid heartbeats, fatigue, confusion, and diz-
ziness settle in, disaster could be imminent. That's exactly where
we find Peter in this text, according to Jesus: "I tell you, Peter, the
rooster will not crow this day, until you deny three times that you
know me" (Luke 22:34).

We knew that there was something wrong when Jesus flagged

him as "Simon" for being fleshly. Also alarming was the fact Peter had no fear of going to war with Satan. But to "deny three times that you know me"—that's as far as a believer can go without falling off the cliff of apostasy. And of course, what became clear that fateful night is not that Peter held Peter, but that Jesus did. When the Savior said, "I have prayed for you that your faith may not fail" (verse 32), we are given assurance that the all-sufficient Christ would not let this self-sufficient Christian be undone. Still, this unprepared disciple would soon see how dark his heart truly was. Matthew recounts the story:

> Now Peter was sitting outside in the courtyard. And a servant girl came up to him and said, "You also were with Jesus the Galilean." But he denied it before them all, saying, "I do not know what you mean" [*that's one*]. And when he went out to the entrance, another servant girl saw him, and she said to the bystanders, "This man was with Jesus of Nazareth." And again he denied it with an oath: "I do not know the man" [*that's two*]. After a little while the bystanders came up and said to Peter, "Certainly you too are one of them, for your accent betrays you." Then he began to invoke a curse on himself and to swear, "I do not know the man" [*that's three; cue the rooster*]. And immediately the rooster crowed. And Peter remembered the saying of Jesus, "Before the rooster crows, you will deny me three times." And he went out and wept bitterly (Matthew 26:69-75).

When the text says Peter "began to invoke a curse on himself," it doesn't mean that he dropped an expletive. It means he said, in essence, "Let me go to hell if I know that man!" Pretty dark. Luke tells us that at this moment, Jesus turned His bruised face toward Peter and singled him out with His puffy eyes. The shrill call of the cockcrow announced that Peter had done what he thought he was incapable of doing, what he boasted everyone else would do before he would. His exterior was crushed, everything that had propped him up was cut down, and the image he had of himself was blown away. Peter had spun out.

Don't Run Over Your Pit Crew

If you retrace Peter's route before his big crash, you will find another obvious defect in his emotional and mental state: his attitude toward the other disciples. This was unmistakable in Jesus's words to Peter, if you read them in the original Greek language:

> "Simon, Simon [*singular, individually*], behold, Satan demanded to have you [*plural, all*], that he might sift you [*plural, all*] like wheat, but I have prayed for you [*singular, you individually*] that your [*singular, individual*] faith may not fail. And when you [*singular, you individually*] have turned again, strengthen your brothers [*plural, all*]" (emphasis added).

Did you follow that? "Simon Peter, it starts with you. You're the leader of this group. Satan wants to sift not only you personally, but all of you. But I have prayed for you, specifically you, for the durability of your faith, that it not unravel. And you, Simon, once you come back from your departure, I want you to build up these other men. Get ready to lead."

But Peter wasn't interested in guiding those under his influence toward spiritual victory; he was focused only on himself. When you compare Luke's account with the other Gospels, you learn that Peter totally ran over his pit crew:

> Jesus said to them, "You will all fall away because of me this night. For it is written, 'I will strike the shepherd, and the sheep of the flock will be scattered.' But after I am

raised up, I will go before you to Galilee." Peter answered him, "*Though they all fall away because of you*, I will never fall away." Jesus said to him, "Truly, I tell you, this very night, before the rooster crows, you will deny me three times" (Matthew 26:30-34, emphasis added).

Instead of seizing the moment to brace himself and lead his brothers, Peter plowed right into them, ruining everyone's hope for victory. With unguarded brashness, in an attempt to make himself seem strong, competent, and committed, he openly declared his friends to be weak, inept, and untrustworthy. In truth, he taught us that we are at our weakest when we think we are at our strongest.

One reason Peter was sifted is so that he could become a stronger and more useful leader, which he aspired to be. But before God could work *through* Peter, He had to work *in* Peter. First God works *in* us, then *through* us—always in that order.

There are drivers who, during a race, have entered pit road too carelessly and smashed into their crew, hurling them into the air. That's something you never want to do to the guys on your team. You need them, and they need you. But sometimes we view them as irritants who are slowing us down. We become so confident in our abilities that we push our pit crew members out of the way. When we do, we hurt ourselves and others. We can never expect to enjoy the victory lap if we disregard our team.

Take Your Victory Lap After You Win

Every first-place winner celebrates his victory differently. Most jump on the roof of their car and pump their fist in the air. Some have been known to climb the fence in front of their fans. Some do backflips, uncork champagne bottles, or burn donuts on the infield grass. But every champ takes a lap around the track, called a victory lap. As he does this, he experiences the wonderful emotion of relief that comes with releasing the tension that had been building for some 240 minutes, the euphoria that every driver who gets behind the wheel longs to enjoy.

But Peter took his victory lap before the sifting was over. His bold "I will never fall away" was, in fact, the beginning of his fall (Matthew 26:33). His promise to the Lord, "Even if I must die with you, I will not deny you!" (verse 35), afforded him a view of the stadium from the back of a tow truck. Never say never. It can happen to you.

We have seen countless examples of athletes celebrating too early and repeating the folly of the hare against the tortoise: Running backs who spiked the football one yard from the end zone, basketball players that didn't guard the half-court shot of the other team in the last second, and sprinters who coronated themselves with the fans' applause while the underdog surged forward and hit the tape first. No contest is immune, and that applies to the Christian life as well. To err is human, but to take your victory lap before the race ends is just plain foolish.

Don't get me wrong. Celebrating victory is a good thing. Thoughts of winning stir motivation. But for us as Christians, our victory lap comes at the end of the race, which is heaven. That is when and where we can revel in the bliss of finishing strong. The moral of Simon Peter's story can be summed up by the words the apostle Paul wrote in 1 Corinthians 10:12: "Therefore let anyone who thinks that he stands take heed lest he fall."

The disasters that took place that Thursday night were compounded by the unbearable agony of the cross on Friday morning. In his epistle, Peter referred to himself as "a witness of the sufferings of Christ" (1 Peter 5:1), which I take to mean that he had a safe perch from which to see Jesus dying on the cross. Peter's guilt must have been unbearable. Little did he know, however, that his sin would be used of God to fulfill a plan that would bring heaven and earth together (see Acts 2:23; 1 Timothy 2:5-6).

The good news was that (1) the cross was God's rescue mission for sinners like Peter (and us); (2) Jesus had prayed for Peter, so this was not the end; and (3) Jesus was going to rise again. The cross was where Jesus would secure our victory, and His resurrection would open the way for Peter—and us—to begin anew.

How to Begin Anew

The Sunday morning after the cross seemed to begin the way Friday ended: another unthinkable tragedy. *The body of Jesus is missing? There was an earthquake? Something about angels?* Peter's footrace with John to the garden tomb confirmed that what the women had said was true, but nothing prepared him for what he would experience when Jesus miraculously appeared in the room where he and the other apostles were huddled together in fear (John 20:19-21). The risen Christ's words, "Peace be with you," were meant to be calming, but they could not remove the shame Peter felt. When Jesus's eyes, no longer slits on a bloody face, met Peter's, I'm sure Peter was the first one to break eye contact. Jesus was alive, just as He had promised, and Simon was more than a colossal disappointment; he was a traitor. "Let me go to hell if I know that man!" replayed in his mind over and over again. He was probably thinking, *Jesus is done with me. It's over. I am going back to my old life.*

Not so fast.

The next time we see Jesus with Peter, it is as the Shepherd coming for His lost sheep on the northern shore of the Sea of Galilee.

Peter was with six other disciples, and rather than strengthening them, as Jesus had instructed him to do, he said to them, "I am going fishing," and they followed him. Understand, Peter was not trying to catch a quick bite. He was returning to the only life he knew, the one thing he was good at. Except this time, he wasn't even good at fishing anymore: "They went out and got into the boat, but that night they caught nothing" (John 21:3).

Then Jesus, who was standing on the shore watching, said,

> "Children, do you have any fish?" They answered him, "No." He said to them, "Cast the net on the right side of the boat, and you will find some." So they cast it, and now they were not able to haul it in, because of the quantity of fish. That disciple whom Jesus loved therefore said to Peter, "It is the Lord!" When Simon Peter heard that it was the Lord, he put on his outer garment, for he was stripped for work, and threw himself into the sea (verses 5-7).

Notice how Peter, despite what he had said and done, was irresistibly drawn to Christ. He had to be near Him. Earlier on this same sea, in a storm, Peter had walked on water to be with Him. In Gethsemane, Peter was willing to take down an entire band of Roman soldiers because they threatened to take his Messiah away. And here, even guilt and shame could not suppress the longing Peter had for Jesus, which the Lord had prayed would remain. So there was Peter, rushing toward Jesus. He didn't know what was coming next, but he knew that Jesus was the answer.

And Jesus was not standing on the beach with His arms crossed, foot tapping, and lip curled, saying, "You foolish disciples, slow to believe, and hard of heart. How could you? After all I've done for you…" Instead, He made breakfast for them on a charcoal fire and ate a meal with them (John 21:9). Charcoal was not commonly used in ancient times—fires were kindled with wood. I believe Jesus did this because in John 18:18, Peter's denials happened while he warmed himself by a "charcoal fire." It seems that Jesus was recreating the scene from Thursday night, when Peter was sifted. The smell of charcoal would have caused a pungent sting in Peter's nostrils. Without a word, Peter and Jesus were instantly transported back to that terrible night to live it again. But Jesus was not rubbing Peter's nose in his sin. He was restoring him back to fellowship and ministry, and in so doing, showing us how we can begin anew, even after we have crashed and burned.

If you have spun out or crashed, this is what you should do:

Get Back in Your Car

If you are in Christ, nothing will ever separate you from His love (Romans 8:37-39). There is nothing you have done or ever will do that will cause Him to break His commitment to you. Your debt has been paid in full. The victory has already been won, by Him. So get back in your car. Jesus made this point after breakfast when He asked, "Simon, son of John, do you love me more than these?" Peter said, "Yes, Lord; you know that I love you." Jesus then responded, "Feed my lambs" (John 21:15).

I am sure it stung worse than the charcoal to hear "Simon" instead of Peter again—a reminder that he was still in his flesh. But Peter was also met with an imperative from his Master: "Feed my lambs." No more fishing; he was to be shepherding! *What are you doing outside of your car? Get back in.* How wonderfully unexpected and hopeful. Jesus was not done with Peter, just like He is not done with you or me. Even when we have been at our absolute worst in the presence of Jesus, He steps toward us to lift us from our past failures.

Start Moving Forward Slowly

Jesus's question, repeated three times, once for each denial, is a question about the fuel that powers Peter forward: "Do you love me?" (John 21:15-17). The Greek language captures what could easily get lost in our English translations. When Jesus asked, "Do you love me more than these?" in verse 15, He used the famous term *agape*. Agape love is the love of choice, the selfless, sacrificial, commitment of unswerving devotion to always do what is in the best interest of another. Jesus asked Peter if that was what he had in his heart for Him. What could Peter say? "Oh yes, of course I do! You are my highest priority—I would die for You." No, he could not say that. His actions had already betrayed him. So Peter used a lesser word: *phileo,* which is the love of friendship and affection, and when used in contrast to agape, speaks of a lesser quality. It's like saying, "I cannot say I love you, but I sure like you a lot."

Jesus came back a second time, "Do you [*agape*] me?" to which Peter replied as before: "Yes Lord; you know that I [at least like] you" (John 21:16). Not quite finished, Jesus asked a third time, "Simon, son of John, do you love me?" but this time Jesus didn't use *agape*; He used Peter's word, *phileo,* as if to say, "Are you sure you really even like Me?"

If Jesus had asked me that, I would have jumped back into the lake instead of answering this final question. Yet though Peter was grieved, he insisted, "Lord, you know everything; you know that I [at least like] you" (John 21:17).

As a believer, despite the pain of falling short in your love for Jesus, like Peter, you do love Him. Your level of love may not be what you want it to be, but you do have a love for Him that can never be put out. You may have to appeal to His omniscience for evidence of it, like Peter did, but your love for Him is real and inextinguishable.

And there is our new starting line: love for Christ, however small and inadequate it may seem.

Very simply, beginning again after a crash-and-burn experience means returning to your first love. You do not have to make sweeping promises that you know you cannot keep, promises that you will do better next time to show Jesus how committed you are. Just love Him. Start moving forward slowly with love as your fuel.

Stick with the Fundamentals

Once you are behind the wheel again and moving forward, keep to the basics of driving: both hands on the wheel, accelerate, brake, left turn, and repeat. Resist the urge to do anything fancy, tricky, or showy. Gain speed slowly and do not worry about who is in the lead. Remember, the victory is already won.

The risen Christ reinstated Peter and graciously reissued His first call three times, once for each dastardly denial: "Feed my lambs...tend my sheep...feed my sheep" (John 21:15-17). Our Lord kept it clear and simple: For the rest of his life, Peter had one divine imperative—to shepherd God's flock. According to Jesus, if Peter could remember that, he could finish well:

> "Truly, truly, I say to you, when you were young, you used
> to dress yourself and walk wherever you wanted, but when
> you are old, you will stretch out your hands, and another
> will dress you and carry you where you do not want to go."
> (This he said to show by what kind of death he was to glo-
> rify God) (John 21:18-19).

Unlike Peter, you and I do not have the luxury of knowing when and exactly how we will die, but just like Peter, we can choose to begin again, knowing that in the end, we can "glorify God." Jesus promised Peter that he would finish strong and be faithful to the end, dying a martyr's death, which he once boasted he would willingly do. Historical traditions unite in saying that Peter indeed died by crucifixion, as did his wife, but that he asked to be crucified upside-down because he was unworthy to die in the same manner as his Lord. He finished well! He got a second chance, and when the time came, he stood for Christ and gave his life for the glory of God.

Stay Focused on Your Own Race

The encounter on the beach was the pivot point for Peter, his U-turn. His failure was erased, his love was rekindled, his calling was reinstated, and his future was ensured. But Peter needed one more lesson, which we would do well to heed. After the news of how Peter would die, Jesus apparently turned around and started walking to draw out a point:

> [Jesus] said to him, "Follow me." Peter turned and saw the disciple whom Jesus loved following them, the one who also had leaned back against him during the supper and had said, "Lord, who is it that is going to betray you?" When Peter saw him, he said to Jesus, "Lord, what about this man?" Jesus said to him, "If it is my will that he remain until I come, what is that to you? You follow me!" (John 21:19-22).

John the apostle wanted to hear what Jesus was saying to Peter. Peter was probably still reeling from having been told he was going to die a gruesome death, and as he looked back to see John eavesdropping on their conversation, Peter wanted to know John's fate. *How would he finish? What was God's will for John's life? Who would be greater?* The answer Peter got was a nonanswer, and in its place, a

Jesus, our champion, is now standing on the platform as the flagman. With His checkered flag in one hand and a green flag in the other, He is waving both of them to us. **It is time to buckle the harness, strap on the helmet, turn on the ignition, step on the gas, and keep going to the very end.**

stern warning to not become distracted by someone else's driving. Peter needed to focus on his own race. It is tempting, and it will be for the rest of our lives, to take our eyes off Christ and put them on others around us.

Single-mindedness was something Peter had to learn over and over again. But once he got it, he became a pillar (Galatians 2:9). This broken man, remade and whole, preached the gospel, refuted false teaching, confronted sinful hearts, led thousands to Christ, shepherded churches, raised up leaders, guided Mark to write his Gospel, and wrote two epistles that ministered to other sifted believers who needed strengthening against the world and the devil. Peter was used mightily by God *after* his spinout.

What was the key to his usefulness? Sifting. Peter was broken down so that he could be built up again, God's way. The once-proud disciple was shown his inadequacy so that he might showcase Christ's sufficiency. God worked *in* Peter personally so that He could work *through* him powerfully. And in using Satan to expose what Peter really was, Jesus made Peter what he hoped he would be. His story is a testimony to this glorious truth: Anyone can finish well.

Keep Going to the Very End

The truth is, all of us have wrecked our lives more times than we can count. While this book has taught you some important truths about going hard and the desperate need for a solid pit crew, the gospel teaches us that victory is found in Christ alone, who has already won the race for us. Jesus has already been exalted in the winner's circle with trophy in hand, and is ready to share it with us. His victory is our victory.

As we await that moment, every day is a new start for us—a new lap. The amazing truth about racing is that the starting line is also the finish line. We begin where Jesus finished. The checkered flag has already waved, but Jesus, our champion, is now standing on the platform as the flagman. With His checkered flag in one hand and a green flag in the other, He is waving both of them to us. It is time to buckle the harness, strap on the helmet, turn on the ignition, step on the gas, and keep going to the very end.

Appendixes

What About the Difficult Men in Our Lives?

In this book, we have looked at ways to become the man God intends by cultivating strategic and godly friendships. These men are often missing from our lives, and they are definitely needed in our quest for spiritual growth and victory. The strength of our manhood and the effectiveness of our leadership will likely rise or fall depending on the men in our pit crews. Which is why you want to choose your guy friends wisely.

Before we close, however, let me pose a question about the guys in our lives who are the opposite of those who are in our pit crews. Each of us has negative men in our lives as well—men who, for one reason or another, are difficult to avoid. In sharp contrast to the friends we need, there are certain kinds of guys we don't really want to have around because they distract and drain us, or in some cases, they spurn and betray us. They give us bad gas mileage and hinder us as we try to win the race.

What should you do when you have to deal with these kinds of guys?

As you probably know, the Bible says that God can use the negative people and experiences in your life to make you more like Christ. You may not have sought their friendship, but God knows that you can come away with useful life lessons from them. That being the case, maybe you should not steer clear of them just yet. Quite possibly, your detractors are tools in God's hand for building up your character and holiness. Consider the following biblical example of a difficult man who was determined to make life as difficult as possible for someone else.

The Deranged Lunatic with the Power Tie

We have all seen this man, and we don't know how anyone works with him. If you've ever met one, you will bristle with the description: a self-centered, self-absorbed alpha male who sits in a position of authority, is thoroughly preoccupied with his own image, feeds on the admiration of others, and behaves with such entitlement that he cannot see past his own ambitions. Such a man, in a word, is dangerous—a ticking time bomb.

Most of us get away from ticking time bombs as fast as we can. But what if you cannot? What if he holds a position of authority over you? Such was the case with David and his cowardly, jealous, angry, demonic king—Saul. As Israel's first king, Saul won the people's choice award in Israel as a strong, natural leader, but he was not God's pick. He was hateful, malicious, irrational, murderous, unpredictable, power hungry, and disobedient. It did not take long for God to reject him and make way for a better man, David. But Saul refused to go down without a fight.

David and Saul first met in the Valley of Elah, where the teenage sheepherder decapitated the most feared man on the planet, Goliath. Saul wanted proximity to David in the same way that all strong leaders want access to heroes. But shortly after Saul welcomed David into the royal family, he was already plotting to bury him next to Goliath. The day Saul turned on David was after he heard the chorus of Israel's new favorite song, "Saul has struck down his thousands, and David his ten thousands" (1 Samuel 18:7). David was a better man, with better character, and better success. Jealousy enslaved and enraged Saul, but that was not the only thing raging inside of him:

> Now it came about on the next day that an evil spirit from God came mightily upon Saul, and he raved in the midst of the house, while David was playing the harp with his hand, as usual; and a spear was in Saul's hand. Saul hurled the spear for he thought, "I will pin David to the wall." But David escaped from his presence twice (1 Samuel 18:10-11 NASB).

The jealous king had a demon who maliciously and frequently took control of his already depraved faculties and turned loose on Saul like a flamethrower in a gunpowder factory. The more David escaped, the more fearful Saul became of David: "Saul was afraid of David because the LORD was with him" (verse 12). The faster David's fame grew, the faster Saul's fear became enmity: "Saul was even more afraid of David. So Saul was David's enemy continually" (verse 29). Saul was a living nightmare, but this was not a dream, and it didn't last only one night. This terror lasted 12 years, from the day Samuel anointed David king to the day the crown rested on his head. But Saul was exactly the kind of man that David needed in his life to move him from being a *man* after God's own heart to becoming a *king* after God's own heart.

Resist the Temptation to Retaliate

Here we learn God's purpose in allowing difficult people into our lives—they teach us something we cannot learn when we are insulated and comfortable. With that in mind, our goal, then, is not *How do I get away from this person?* Rather, we should ask, *What does God want to teach me in this season through this person?* If you know guys who are making life difficult by their opposition or intimidation, resist the temptation to retaliate, and instead, let the lessons to be learned stretch you as well.

Patience

Our favorite lesson, right? Patience is the one thing people tell us to never pray for, because you will get it. But let's get real practical and uncomfortable: In the midst of this crazy rerun of Looney Tunes, David was submissive to Saul. Wherever Saul sent him, David went and prospered. This, of course, made Saul rage against him all the more. But just as fast as Saul was to turn on David, Saul was quick to promote him too: "Saul was afraid of David because the LORD was with him but had departed from Saul. So Saul removed him from his presence and made him a commander of a thousand. And he went out and came in before the people" (1 Samuel 18:12-13).

Makes perfect sense, right? *Kill him! That didn't work. Promote him! That backfired—now David is greater than ever. Kill him again!*

David's story proves that you can be whacked all over the place like a pinball by the whims of a psychotic person, and God can still give you the grace to be long-suffering and endure with the right attitude. But this works only when you remember this: It is not about that guy—not yet. Rather, it's about you and what God wants to do to make you holier. And that won't happen overnight. Learning patience, by definition, takes time—sometimes as long as 12 years.

Humility

One of Saul's empty promises and manipulative tricks against David was the offer of one of his daughters to become David's wife. At first David was supposed to marry Merab, but on their wedding day, the king, out of spite, snatched her away and gave her to another man. To save face and set a subtler trap, Saul suggested another daughter, Michal, who actually loved David. But Saul required David to go out and kill 100 Philistines to prove his worthiness of her. Saul's secret aim was to have David killed by the Philistines, who were still upset about losing their best fighter, Goliath. *One giant—meh, that was a lucky shot. One hundred men, he's a goner.*

Astonishingly, rather than storm off, cry foul, or jump ship, David stayed in the conflict and showed self-effacing humility. We see this in David's response to the men who enticed him to take the deal: "Does it seem to you a little thing to become the king's son-in-law, since I am a poor man and have no reputation?" (1 Samuel 18:23). All David could think about, on the same day that his fiancé was ripped away from him, was how unworthy he was to even be offered the privileges he had been given. It was not about David.

What should you do when you encounter an arrogant, selfish, insecure person? Be the opposite in return. How could David do that, and why would he? He did it because he realized that ultimately, all authority comes from God, who is fully sovereign over all things and people (see Romans 13:1-5). Though Saul was evil, it was God who "anointed" him to reign as David's king, and that made Saul worthy of respect and honor. Even if the authority figures in your life aren't worthy of the honor that comes with their position, you can honor them as long as they are in that position because God put them there. In the meantime, trust God to take care of you in His perfect timing and provision.

Integrity

There was a day that David could have ended the torture Saul was inflicting upon him. David was on the run and chose to hide with his men in the caves of Engedi, a lush oasis in the midst of a bleak desert, just a short distance away from the Dead Sea. It was the perfect place to go, as it provided enough shade and water to refresh his men and enough caves to hide, by some estimates, more than 30,000 men.

King Saul and his soldiers, bent on destroying David, heard he was there, and scoured the caves. In one of the most awkward but providential incidents in the Bible, King Saul walked into the exact cave where David and his men were hiding in order "to relieve himself" (1 Samuel 24:3). Saul was using the cave as a squatty potty, only feet away from David, leaving Saul completely vulnerable and giving David the perfect opportunity to eliminate his foe, who would never see it coming.

We have no idea how tempting this was for David. The hunt for his life would have been over and his problems solved. He could have returned to Jerusalem, assumed the throne, and stopped this reign of terror against himself and his 600 men. Think about it: No more living on the run or hiding in caves. He could go home, sleep in his own bed, eat at his own table, and no one would have blamed him. All he had to do was sin by taking Saul's life.

This moment begs the question: What if you knew that you could get out of the most difficult situation in your life by one simple act of compromise? Would you do it? It might have to do with your marriage relationship, an unwise business venture, or a financial crisis. You know that if you were to compromise in a way that few others would see, the results would turn out to your advantage. Your answer reveals how much integrity you have. David could not do it:

> David arose and stealthily cut off a corner of Saul's robe. And afterward David's heart struck him, because he had cut off a corner of Saul's robe. He said to his men, "The LORD forbid that I should do this thing to my lord, the LORD's anointed, to put out my hand against him, seeing he is the LORD's anointed." So David persuaded his men with these words and did not permit them to attack Saul. And Saul rose up and left the cave and went on his way (1 Samuel 24:4-7).

Amazingly, David chose character over relief. He had too much integrity, and yet even in his restraint, "David's heart struck him" because he had cut off the corner of Saul's robe. We would be tempted to think David was being a little imbalanced in his view of integrity. He could have congratulated himself for overcoming the temptation to kill the king and shooed away the little fly buzzing around his conscience, but David knew his own heart. That he had cut the corner of Saul's robe wasn't a meaningless act. In ancient Israel, when Jews were buried, they were laid in their tombs, covered with their prayer shawls, and a corner was cut off the shawl to symbolize that they were cut off from of the land of the living. David wasn't merely snipping off the president's tie, as it were—he was saying, in effect, "You are a dead man." He had gone too far, which explains what he did next:

> Afterward David also arose and went out of the cave, and called after Saul, "My lord the king!" And when Saul looked behind him, David bowed with his face to the earth and paid homage. And David said to Saul, "Why do you listen to the words of men who say, 'Behold, David seeks your harm'? Behold, this day your eyes have seen how the LORD gave you today into my hand in the cave. And some told me to kill you, but I spared you. I said, 'I will not put out my hand against my lord, for he is the LORD's anointed.' See, my father, see the corner of your robe in my hand. For by the fact that I cut off the corner of your robe and did not kill you, you may know and see that there is no wrong or treason in my hands. I have not sinned against you, though you hunt my life to take it. May the LORD judge between me and you, may the LORD avenge me against you, but my hand shall not be against you" (verses 8-12).

What was David doing? If he felt bad about cutting the robe, fine—pray to God and ask for forgiveness. But do not go outside, do not reveal yourself to your murderer, and *definitely* do not kneel down before him! He did not have to do these things. The worst was already past—no one would have searched that cave looking for David because Saul had already been in it. David was home free. But God kept pricking David's heart. Rather that delivering himself by compromise, David valued the freedom of his conscience over freedom from his circumstances. He respected God's authority over man's opinions and acted according to principle rather than impulse. As a result of his integrity, God delivered David time and time again, until his vindication on the sober day of Saul's demise.

That day of vindication is coming for you as well. Hold fast to your integrity, wait on the Lord, and stay low.

Let God Do His Work in Your Life

God will deal with your enemies in His own time and His own way. He will move you out of the difficult situations you are in when He is ready. Until that happens, God is doing something in your heart that cannot happen if you take the easy way out. How should you handle a Saul? Let God take care of him—He will.

What About Your Wife?

Every Christian man needs other men in his life to come alongside him at different times and for different purposes. As this book has shown, you should strive to develop and deepen godly friendships with other men so that you can become all that God intends. While it may be ideal to have each of these seven relationships healthy and strong at all times for the rest of your life, it's probably more likely that you will have certain friendships during seasons when you most need them. That seems like the biblical pattern.

For example, David had Jonathan while God was preparing him to be king through trial by fire. Then just like that, Jonathan was gone. When David died, Nathan had to start again with a new king. Timothy had to come to grips with the fact Paul was going to die. Then it would be Timothy's turn to be a Paul. Paul would say a remorseful goodbye to his ministry partner Barnabas after a conflict broke apart their 17-year friendship, with the result they would never work together again. And there will always be a Zacchaeus who needs Christ, and the opportunity to invite yourself over for dinner.

Realistically, friendships don't last forever. Not in this life. Also, no friendship is perfect. In fact, they can get quite messy. Friendships take a lot of hard work. Each of the men described in this book got to enjoy the benefits of their friendships when it mattered most, but there may come times when we experience conflict or we move on to other friendships for one reason or another.

In the course of reading this book, you may have wondered, *What about my wife?* In chapter 1, as you read about how Paul mentored Timothy, you may have thought about the fact that God designed your wife to speak into your life as well. When you saw the pattern of discipleship in Timothy, no doubt you felt the responsibility of spiritually investing in your bride first, before discipling anyone outside your marriage and family. As you read the description of a best friend as exemplified by Jonathan, you may have considered the fact that God wants your wife to be your best friend. As you looked at the ministry partnership between Paul and Barnabas, hopefully you thought about how to be a team with your bride in ministry. As you considered the way Nathan courageously battled for David's repentance, perhaps you recalled times when your wife urged you toward holiness in your own life. If your wife is not a Christian, then as you read about Jesus's pursuit of Zacchaeus, you may have felt impassioned about seeing salvation come to your house before you attempt to bring it to someone else's house. And if your wife is a Christian, you know that in terms of your ministry to others, she and your family come first.

So how does everything we've seen in this book fit together with your marriage? Your relationship with your wife is not meant to be for a season, it's for life. And while marriages too can get messy and are sometimes cut short, our God-given union is not meant to compete with the friendships described in the Bible. They fit hand in glove.

To start, we need to recognize that when God said, "It is not good for the man to be alone" (Genesis 2:18), He was making it clear that Adam, on his own, was incomplete. Note that everything God had made during the six days of creation was "good" (Genesis 1:31). Now, as Adam named the animals, it was evident they all had partners, but that wasn't true about Adam. Thus God declared, "I will make him a helper fit for him" (2:18). Adam needed a companion, someone to complete him and fill in his gaps—a suitable helper. In His perfect wisdom, God gave Adam a woman to be his lifelong partner, not male friends or companions. He brought Adam and Eve together in blissful oneness with the gift called marriage.

Guy friends may interact with us, but our wives are always with us. Our wives know us intimately, unlike another man. Other men may help us, but they are not our "helpers." They might mean well, but they can never ultimately become "one" with us as a woman was designed to do. Every aspect of your being as a man was created to fit together with every aspect of her being as a wife. Another man is not supposed to encroach on that intimacy.

What great helpers our wives are if we let them fulfill their God-given roles. Emotionally, we need our wives to nurture us as we share our joys and sorrows—guys can't do that like our wives can. Mentally, we depend on our wives to counterbalance our thinking with their perspective, like other men cannot because they think like men. Spiritually, we bond with our wives together before God and become soul mates—everything we believe forms the deepest convictions of life and is the basis for our morality and motivation.

And of course, physically, we need our wives to satisfy us with the intimacy of their touch, as we do them, only.

The point is this: The men in our lives can only take us so far. Your wife is the primary tool God uses for your good and your growth.

This also means that as good and powerful as male relationships can be, they still leave us with gaps that only our wives can fill. By God's design, we are very much incomplete. He made women to complement us in ways that other men cannot possibly fulfill, far beyond procreation. There are certain places that a man should not go with another man relationally; those are the exclusive right of his wife.

So everything you have studied about your friendships with other men should be true of your relationship with your wife, and much more so. Other men should never take her place. And yet, as demonstrated in each chapter, God has a role for each of those men that we cannot do without, even as married men.

What's the balance? Think of your wife as being like a Leatherman Supertool 300. Google it if you don't know what I'm talking about. It has every tool for every job. That's your wife: always with you, fit for every situation, versatile, strong, trustworthy, and enjoyable to look at. You can handle most jobs with a Supertool 300. But on occasion you might encounter a screw that is stripped, a rope too thick to be cut, or a bolt that is too big, and you will need the leverage offered by a niche tool. That's where your male friends step in, to do the refining work with the support of your wife. She may recognize those times when you need the help of a man, and free you to seek just that.

As your life partner, your wife should be the one whose counsel and wisdom you seek most often. Yet she will also recognize when you receive the input and guidance of another man who has been where you have not, then not only do you benefit—she does as well. As one who has benefited from you discipling and building her up spiritually in the marriage relationship, she will want to share you with other men whom you can disciple—men who can pass on the same legacy in their own homes and lives. That will be joyful for her.

When it comes to confrontation, sometimes it's going to be better for you to "take it like a man" from another man. You need someone whom you cannot intimidate physically or manipulate using Ephesians 5:22-24—someone who is willing to get in your face and tell you what you don't want to hear.

In your ministry partnerships and in your closest male friendships, you and your wife both know that guys understand guys in certain areas where women don't totally relate. Certain men can strengthen and sharpen us in ways our wives cannot. Our wives should encourage us to develop the kinds of male friendships that equip us to become the man God wants us to be.

My guess is that your wife will not be against any of the relationships mentioned in this book. She will be the first and most direct beneficiary of them. The more those men help you grow, the more she will gain. If there's any place where she might object, it's going to be when you let those relationships replace her special role in your life. Don't cultivate your male friendships at her expense. Rather, make sure you view your friendships as the overflow of a healthy relationship with your wife. If your relationship with your wife becomes unhealthy, then your friends should do you the favor of helping to strengthen your relationship with your wife. She is your first priority, after your relationship with Jesus.

Now that you're done with this book, if you're married, you may want to pass it on to your wife and let her read it. Encourage her to find the same kinds of relationships with other women, and to make room for your relationship with these kinds of men. Then go out and buy a Leatherman Supertool 300 and tell your wife it's a biblical reminder to you of the special place she has in your life.

Notes

1. John MacArthur, *Ashamed of the Gospel: When the Church Becomes Like the World* (Wheaton, IL: Crossway Books, 1993), 25.

2. John Piper, "Going Hard After the Holy God," https://www.desiringgod.org/messages/going-hard-after-the-holy-god.

3. Some have attributed this prayer to Saint Patrick, but the actual source of origin is uncertain.

4. Benjamin Garniss O'Rorke, *African Missions Impressions of the South, East, and Centre of the Dark Continent* (London: Society for Promoting Christian Knowledge, 1912), 65.

5. Steve Miller, *C.H. Spurgeon on Spiritual Leadership* (Chicago, IL: Moody Publishers, 2003), 166.

6. Abby Stocker, "The Craziest Statistic You'll Read About North American Missions," https://www.christianitytoday.com/ct/2013/august-web-only/non-christians-who-dont-know-christians.html.

7. John Styles, *David Brainerd, Missionary to the Indians with an Abridgment of His Diary and Journals from President Edwards* (Boston, MA: Samuel T. Armstrong, 1812), 80.

8. For examples, see: Luke 11:5-13; 14:7-11; 16:9.

9. For examples of the word "servant" or "bondservant" used in the New Testament, as used to describe our relationship to God, see 1 Corinthians 7:21; Ephesians 6:6; James 1:1. For a more in-depth study of the concept of slavery as a metaphor for the Christian life, see John MacArthur. *Slave* (Nashville, TN: Thomas Nelson, 2010).

10. Isaac Watts, "When I Survey the Wondrous Cross," written in 1707, http://library.timelesstruths.org/music/When_I_Survey_the_Wondrous_Cross.

Other Good Harvest House Reading

Men of the Word

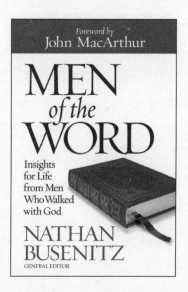

NATHAN BUSENITZ, GENERAL EDITOR

What is God's calling for men? What character qualities does He value? What is biblical manhood, and how is it cultivated?

The answers to those all-important questions are found in the lives of men of the Bible—men like Abraham, Joseph, Moses, Joshua, Daniel, and Paul. Every one of them struggled with the same issues faced by men today…which makes them highly relevant role models that define what a real man is from God's perspective.

You will discover that real men...

- treasure God's Word
- refuse to compromise
- wait on the Lord
- pray with boldness
- lead with courage
- reflect God's love
- serve with humility
- count the cost

This resource is both powerful and down-to-earth practical, providing much-needed clarity and encouragement on the essentials of biblical manhood. Men will find great fulfillment as they pursue all that God desires for them to be.

Right Thinking in a World Gone Wrong

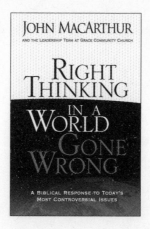

One of the greatest challenges facing Christians today is the powerful influence of secular thinking. From all directions we're fed a constant barrage of persuasive—yet unbiblical—worldviews. This makes it difficult to know where to stand on today's most talked-about issues.

The leadership team at Grace Community Church, along with their pastor, John MacArthur, provide much-needed discernment and clarity in the midst of rampant confusion. Using the Bible as the foundation, you'll learn how to develop a Christian perspective on key issues—including…

political activism	environmentalism
homosexual marriage	abortion and birth control
euthanasia and suicide	immigration
disasters and epidemics	God and the problem of evil

This guide will arm you with right thinking and biblical answers to challenging questions. About the Author

About the Author

Justin Erickson (MDiv) is a pastor and church planter who is dedicated to teaching, discipling, counseling, and training men into godly relationships. He is the founder of the online ministry website **itstandswritten.org**. Justin and his wife, Jana, are the parents of five children and call Arizona home.

To learn more about Harvest House books and
to read sample chapters, visit our website:

www.harvesthousepublishers.com

HARVEST HOUSE PUBLISHERS
EUGENE, OREGON